You Can Buy Happiness
(and It's Cheap)

You Can Buy Happiness
(and It's Cheap)

How One Woman Radically Simplified Her Life and How You Can Too

Tammy Strobel

New World Library
Novato, California

New World Library
14 Pamaron Way
Novato, California 94949

The material in this book is intended for education. It is not meant to take the place of diagnosis and treatment by a qualified medical practitioner or therapist. No expressed or implied guarantee as to the effects of the use of the recommendations can be given nor liability taken.

Text design by Tona Pearce-Myers

Library of Congress Cataloging-in-Publication Data
Strobel, Tammy, date.
You can buy happiness (and it's cheap) : how one woman radically simplified her life and how you can too / Tammy Strobel.
p. cm.
Includes bibliographical references and index.
ISBN 978-1-60868-083-2 (pbk. : alk. paper)
1. Happiness. 2. Self-actualization (Psychology) 3. Simplicity. I. Title.
BF575.H27S77 2012
650.1—dc23 2012018289

First printing, September 2012
ISBN 978-1-60868-083-2
Printed in Canada on 100% postconsumer-waste recycled paper

New World Library is proud to be a Gold Certified Environmentally Responsible Publisher. Publisher certification awarded by Green Press Initiative. www.greenpressinitiative.org

10 9 8 7 6 5 4 3 2

To the incredible people in my life:
Logan, my life partner and best friend.
Dee Williams, my tiny house hero.
My parents, who have been a constant source of strength,
wisdom, and support.
Thank you for inspiring me every day. I couldn't do this without you.

Contents

Part 3: Buying Happiness

Gratitude

One of the reasons I'm writing this book is because of an article written by Stephanie Rosenbloom that appeared in the *New York Times* business section. My husband, Logan Smith, and I were featured in the article and as a result received a lot of media inquiries. In addition, I was approached by a number of literary agents about writing a book. Writing a book has always been a dream, and I'm thankful that Stephanie happened to Google "simplicity and happiness" and subsequently navigated her way to my blog, RowdyKittens.com.

As Dennis Waitely, a speaker and writer, once said, "Happiness cannot be traveled to, owned, earned, worn or consumed. Happiness is a spiritual experience of living every moment with love, grace and gratitude." With that said, books are not created without a lot of support and encouragement. I couldn't have written this book without the remarkable people mentioned below. I'm extremely grateful for all of their efforts, both large and small.

I'm indebted to my incredible literary agent, David Fugate. He believed in this project from the beginning and was instrumental in helping me shape the ideas presented here. I appreciate David's help, patience, and support.

A huge thanks goes to Jason Gardner, my editor, and the whole team at New World Library. Jason has a keen editorial eye, and he consistently pushed me to do better. I've grown as a writer thanks to his help and encouragement.

Several people served as my cheerleading team as I wrote this book, including Chris O'Byrne, Courtney Carver, Jolie Guillebeau, Dee Williams, and Michelle Jones. They all provided valuable guidance and encouragement when I hit bumps in the road and started to doubt my ability to finish this project.

My family has been a tremendous source of my happiness. I wouldn't be writing today if it weren't for my parents. I owe a huge debt of gratitude to my mom, Kathy, who spent ten years as a single parent, working and raising me. My mom has been an incredible source of inspiration to me, and I love her with all my heart. She met my stepdad, Mahlon, at a pivotal time in my life. Over the years, he was a constant source of wisdom, strength, and support. Sadly, he passed away a few weeks before this book went to print. He was loved and will be missed. My dad, otherwise known as Stormin' Norman, has constantly challenged my ideals by asking hard questions about my life choices.

To all the amazing individuals who let me interview them for this book — thank you. This book wouldn't be the same without your stories.

Another huge thanks goes to the readers of RowdyKittens.com!

Thanks for sticking around for the past four years. I'm deeply appreciative of every click that comes my way and every heartfelt comment that's been left on the blog. Thank you for your support!

Last, but not least, a huge thank you goes to my husband, Logan. I could not have written this book without his constant pep talks and willingness to listen when my confidence faltered. I never imagined that I'd find true love in a bar or get married, but I did. And I couldn't ask for a better best friend and life partner.

INTRODUCTION

Rethinking Normal

Compared to what we ought to be, we are only half awake.

— William James

Have you ever experienced a turning point? Where the tide beneath your feet completely shifts and you start thinking in a brand-new way? On December 31, 2007, I experienced a turning point — an idea that caused me to wake up out of a deep haze. It all started with a short YouTube video featuring Dee Williams. In the video, Dee talked about the idea of downsizing, or what she called "smart-sizing herself," and why she decided to build a small, cozy dwelling on wheels.

After watching the video, I became completely intrigued by the idea of simplifying my life, and subsequently I read other articles about Dee and her little house. In one article, she described a trip she took to Guatemala to help build a school. When she returned home she realized there was a lot of stuff in her life she simply didn't need. In a small zine called *The Little House* Dee described her trip by saying, "I met some incredible people. They were generous and kind and very, very poor. They didn't have running water or electricity in their houses. They cooked outside and shared a bathroom with their neighbors. And still they seemed happy…at least, they made our work fun and helped me feel happy." When Dee returned to Portland, Oregon, she sold her "big house" and decided to downsize dramatically by building her own tiny, 84-square-foot home on wheels, a dwelling similar in size to the homes she saw in Guatemala.

Dee's story resonated with me on a number of levels. She was the kind of person I wanted to be; she prioritized what was most important in life, like building strong relationships, giving back to her community, and doing what she loved for a living. She wasn't focused on the acquisition of material goods and was authentically living her ideals. Most of all, she seemed happy.

Dee's story inspired me to go small and start thinking big. After reading a lot of blogs and books focused on simple living, my husband, Logan, and I decided to start downsizing our living space. We gave away most of our belongings. Interestingly, the more we gave away, the better we felt. Happiness researchers call this a "helper's high," in which helping others through volunteering or giving reduces stress and releases endorphins.

Prior to this turning point, I had been living a "normal life" and I wasn't happy. Logan and I were thirty thousand dollars in debt, living paycheck to paycheck, and felt stuck in a rut. Something had to change, especially if we wanted to make our dreams a reality.

As I was doing background research for this book, I wondered what a "normal life" looked like in the United States. I discovered some very disturbing trends. For instance, in September 2011 the nation's poverty rate rose to 15.1 percent — its highest level in seventeen years. According to the US Census Bureau, household income declined between 2009 and 2011, and the number of people without health insurance increased. In September 2011, National Public Radio reported, "Income declined for just about everyone — surprisingly — at a faster rate overall than it did in 2008, when the recession was in full swing." In addition, a variety of reports indicate the average American carries over eight thousand dollars in credit card debt and has 6.5 credit cards. Like many Americans, Logan and I had good intentions — we wanted to pay down our debt, improve our health, and contribute to our community. Until we made a shift in our lifestyle, none of these things would happen.

Living simply enabled us to make our dreams a reality. The lifestyle changes we made improved our marriage and relationships with friends and family members. For instance, by selling both our cars, we've lost weight — we get around by bicycle now — and we aren't worried about earning enough money to pay for our cars every month. Instead, we used the money we would have spent on car payments to pay down debt.

Where We're Going

In *The Art of Non-conformity*, Chris Guillebeau notes, "I adhere to a guru-free philosophy, I don't claim to have all the answers." I'm on the same page as Chris. I'm not a simplicity or happiness guru, and I don't have all the answers. As an avid reader, I learn the most from stories. During the course of this book, I tell a lot of stories about my life and the lives of the people I interviewed. I provide "micro-actions" for putting the ideas into practice. In addition, I share a number of inspiring lessons I've learned along the way. Those lessons include:

- Happiness comes from connecting to your community and building strong relationships.

- Money can buy happiness, but it depends on how you spend it.
- The excessive consumption of material goods won't make you happy over the long run.
- Learning to get more from less is one way to find happiness, reclaim your time, and live on your own terms.
- Any kind of life change requires hard work, patience, and the willingness to be open to new perspectives.

Throughout this book, we explore these lessons in more detail. In essence, this book is an invitation to rethink your relationship with money, time, and stuff, to reconsider the things that make you happy. This book offers a different perspective, an outlook that encourages you to examine new ideas and options that are different from the norm.

The idea of living with less goes by several names and movements; a few are the simple living movement, the small house movement, voluntary simplicity, downsizing, and minimalism. The main idea behind them is to be intentional about your choices. For instance, to be part of the small house movement, you aren't required to live in a certain-size tiny house. Moving to a small house might be your long-term goal, but you can be part of the community without doing so. Living with less is a life philosophy; it's not about the number of things you own.

Life Is Short

During Christmas of 2010, I stumbled across some old letters from my great-aunt Mamie. Normally, I'm not sentimental about old letters. However, I was happy to find them hidden in my childhood closet.

When I started reading the letters, I got teary eyed because I miss my aunt tremendously. As I was reading, I started thinking about how she constantly challenged societal norms. My aunt lived simply and didn't spend a whole lot of money on unnecessary stuff. In addition, she never married, had children, or owned a car. She loved to travel and took the bus and walked everywhere.

As a result, she was able to take long trips across the country, and she always wrote friends and family detailed letters about her adventures. For a woman who came of age during the Great Depression, these choices were unusual. The cultural norm dictated that she get married and have kids, not travel across the country or move from a small rural town in Washington to the big city of San Francisco.

Through her letters my aunt taught me about happiness, love, and the good life. In one of her letters, she described the seemingly mundane tasks of her everyday life, like watering the flowers, walking to the grocery store, and talking to her neighbors. Toward the end of the letter she wrote a few lines that surprised me. She said, "Remember, Tammy, life is short. Do what you love and help others, too. It's natural to think you'll be happy if you conform to the norm. I don't think that's true. It's okay to be yourself. This is just a small reminder: Don't lose track of your dreams."

I originally received this letter during high school, and her words were what I needed to hear. I wasn't happy and felt depressed because I didn't have a boyfriend and wasn't part of the "cool crowd." I was looking for external validation to prove to myself that I was "normal." Searching for that kind of validation doesn't result in a whole lot of happiness, because no one is "normal."

Yet, the messages you receive from advertisers tell a different story. When I watch television or see ads on the Internet, the messages tell me I need to buy a product to be happy and content and to fit in. Intuitively, I know this isn't true, because happiness can't be bought at the mall. However, advertising can be very persuasive.

Norman MacEwan, an author and scholar, once said, "Happiness is not so much in having as sharing. We make a living by what we get, but we make a life by what we give." MacEwan's quote echoes what my aunt Mamie was trying to get at in her letters. Like my aunt's letters, this book offers alternative viewpoints and stories. I don't want you to sleepwalk through life like I did. I want you to find your own version of happiness. Let's get started!

PART 1

The Paradox of Stuff

CHAPTER 1

Buying Things Will Not Make You Happy

People say we're searching for the meaning of life.
I don't think that's it at all. I think that what we're seeking
is an experience of being alive.

— Joseph Campbell

The metal hangers made a clicking noise as I browsed through the racks of suits. I was with my friend Lisa, and we were out shopping again on our lunch break. I didn't have a lot of professional-looking clothes, and Lisa always looked stylish, so I enlisted her to help me revamp my wardrobe. Besides, shopping on our lunch break was the perfect opportunity to escape "campus."

Campus was what corporate headquarters called our office. There were four huge buildings, and each unit held about four hundred people. The complex had no character and reminded me of a desert because the structures were so lifeless. On the surface it seemed like campus would be brimming with happy people. But that wasn't the case. To escape the environment, Lisa and I would drive to the outlet mall for weekly shopping breaks.

The outlet mall wasn't much better than campus. On the positive side, the mall walkways were lined with a little bit of shrubbery and bright flowers. Despite the bright flowers, the people at the outlet mall seemed to exude negative energy. Everyone was in a hurry. Especially during a sale — it was like being in the middle of an elephant stampede.

I was part of the herd, too, because I only had a limited amount of time to browse the racks. I had to be back in the cubicle forest by one o'clock at the latest. More often than not, I'd buy a cute blouse to go with my suit, and I'd always feel better afterward — at least temporarily. The high I got from my shopping trips didn't last long. I was on what Sonja Lyubomirsky, in *The How of Happiness*, calls the "hedonic treadmill." This isn't the kind of treadmill that helps you get into shape. If you keep running on this treadmill, you'll feel depleted and, more than likely, be saddled with a whole lot of debt and stress. For example, all the new outfits I bought at the outlet mall gave me momentary pleasure, but eventually I adapted to them and got bored with them. Essentially, I wasn't getting a very good return on my investment. I always thought spending money on stuff would make me happy in the long run. However, I was wrong. Research on this topic tells a different story.

Knox College professor Tim Kasser writes in *The High Price of Materialism* that about 35 percent of Americans in 1957 described themselves as "very happy." We haven't reached that level since, and that's surprising, especially since we're making more money than ever and have a plethora of material goods in our homes. Even Americans who have plenty of material wealth aren't as happy as you might think. According to the Happy Planet Index, conducted by the New Economics Foundation, the United States ranks 114 out of 143 countries measured. The Happy Planet Index survey is "an innovative measure that shows the ecological efficiency with which human well-being is delivered around the world. It is the first ever index to combine environmental impact with well-being to measure the environmental efficiency with which, country by country, people live long and happy lives."

Countries like Costa Rica, Malta, and Malaysia, as well as most countries in Europe and all of Latin America, score above the United States. A likely reason for the relative poor performance of the United States is the misplaced emphasis on material wealth as an indicator of well-being.

Extensive research has linked unhappiness and negative emotions with a materialistic mindset. For instance, in 1976, researchers surveyed twelve thousand eighteen-year-old college freshmen and then measured their life satisfaction again at age thirty-seven. The students who expressed materialistic aspirations at age eighteen were less satisfied with their lives twenty years later.

Tim Kasser argues that "strong materialistic values are associated with a pervasive undermining of people's well-being, from low life satisfaction and happiness, to depression and anxiety, to physical problems such as headaches and to personality disorders, narcissism, and antisocial behavior." Kasser points out that these negative outcomes end up fueling more consumption — as was the case for me. In addition, materialistic people hold very high expectations for what their stuff can or should do for them. In short, materialism distracts us from two main facets in life that actually make us happy — strong relationships and doing work you love. The good news is that more and more people are forgoing materialism and choosing to live a simpler life.

Samuel Alexander and Simon Ussher, researchers at a think tank called the Simplicity Institute, conducted a multinational online survey about the voluntary simplicity movement in 2011. They analyzed data from 1,748 respondents who were asked why they chose to live with less and what reasons were behind their decision. Specifically, Alexander and Ussher wanted to see if this group was measurably happier with their own lives. Not surprisingly, the survey participants who voluntarily downsized their stuff, debt, and work commitments were indeed happier. The participants also pointed out that their decision to live simply wasn't all about personal happiness. The group was motivated to simplify their lives because they wanted more time for family and friends, to pursue creative endeavors, and to volunteer in their community.

Overall, 87 percent of survey respondents said they "were happier living simply." Alexander and Ussher pointed out that the "results do not 'prove' that living simply will make a person happier. They do show that the overwhelming majority of participants in this extensive study are notably happier for living more simply." Of course, asking this group if they are "happier" is kind of like asking kids in a candy shop if they like sweets — they're highly likely to say yes. However, the results are intriguing and suggest that opting out of mindless materialism is a good idea, especially when you consider the impact of a consumer-based mindset on kids.

Kathy's Story: Growing Up with Material Wealth

While my mom waited at the top of the staircase, she would twirl her hair and gaze at old wallpaper that depicted a brown monkey jumping from tree to tree. This was part of her weekly routine as a child. She would tiptoe from her bedroom and sit at the top of the stairs waiting for her dad to get home. As she waited she was scared because it was well past her bedtime and getting caught meant she'd be in big trouble. Eventually, her Dad would come home, but she never had the courage to talk to him, which was probably a good thing, because her parents would inevitably start fighting about money.

My mom, Kathy Hettick, was born in 1948 and grew up in Loudonville, New York — a small community nestled in Albany. Her family had everything you could want or need, including boats, cars, a huge two-story house in Loudonville, and two homes on

Lake George. From an outsider's perspective, it looked as if her family had the perfect life.

I still remember the first time I saw her childhood home. My mom and I did a "drive-by" to check it out. The house was huge and reminded me of a movie set. Painted a light blue, with white shutters at the windows, it looked as if June Cleaver should be standing at the front door with a tray of cookies in her hand.

Every time we visited New York my mom explored her old stomping grounds. We'd drive by her childhood home and take a trip to Lake George and look around the now-defunct summer camp she'd attended. The big homes, the fancy cars, the country clubs, and even the Lake George camp for girls were long gone. Yet my mom could still transport herself into the past and revisit the good memories from her childhood, like her mom's beautiful clothes and her dad's sense of humor.

My mom described her mother, Mary Jane, as a "high-society lady, who looked a lot like Elizabeth Taylor." She was tall, had huge blue eyes, and was always dressed perfectly. Mary Jane wore gloves, pearls, and formal three-quarter- or full-length dresses with a decorative trim. My grandfather Lance could have been a stunt double for Jackie Gleason, both in looks and with his bubbly sense of humor. He was a socialite and a businessman, and he loved being around people. Lance and Mary Jane basked in their money. They spent their leisure time playing golf, hanging out at country clubs, or at Lake George. As I talked with my mom about my grandparents, I asked her: "Do you think all of this material wealth made your parents happy? What about you? Were you happy as a kid?"

She told me, "In some ways yes, and in other ways no. Your grandparents drank a lot and fought about money all the time. I think they loved each other in the beginning, but their priorities differed, especially when it came to spending money on stuff and experiences." As my mom explained, "I found this really upsetting, and it didn't make me feel very happy. My basic needs were covered, but the only time I was truly happy as a kid was at summer camp. Going to summer camp and leaving the house saved my life. I think I would have gone crazy without some kind of outlet."

My mom told me during another conversation that Grandpa Lance spent a lot of my grandmother's inherited money. She had roughly a million dollars in a trust fund, which was funneled into Lance's lumber business. My mom explained, "She felt like she was being taken advantage of because your grandfather would be out working all day, and he was rarely home for dinner. After work he would go out drinking at the country club and would flirt with the ladies. The alcohol fueled a lot of arguments over money and their marriage."

My conversations with my mom about her childhood remind me of Madeline Levine's research. She's worked for decades treating unhappy kids and is an expert on how the media influences child development. In *The Price of Privilege*, she argues that "America's newly identified at-risk group is preteens and teens from affluent, well-educated families." She goes on to say, "In spite of their economic and social advantages, they experience among the highest rates of depression, substance abuse, anxiety disorders, somatic complaints, and unhappiness of any group of children in this country." I can see a lot of parallels between the symptoms Levine describes and my mom's childhood. For example, one of my uncles has struggled with alcoholism throughout his life. My mom noted, "After big parties at the lake house my brother cleaned up the mess. He picked up the glasses and drank the leftover booze. He was only twelve years old and that's when his trouble with alcohol began."

The biggest lesson I learned from my mom's story is that growing up with a lot of money isn't necessarily a ticket to a happy life. As a child my mom didn't crave stuff; what she wanted was a strong connection with her parents. In essence, she wanted to be seen and heard.

Jenna's Story: Less Is More

In contrast to my mom's story, Jenna is an only child, and when she was young, her family didn't have a lot of money. However, as Jenna pointed out, they "weren't poor either."

Jenna grew up in the suburbs outside Portland, Oregon, and her mom loved to shop. In fact, she shopped so much that she frequently overcharged her credit cards and bounced checks. Jenna never understood why her mom shopped so much, because she already had a lot of stuff. Most of her closets were packed with clothing, shoes, and luggage, and the bathroom cabinets were bursting with cosmetics.

Growing up, Jenna said, "I always felt like our house was dirty because stuff ended up being strewn about the house in big piles. The piles were endless — nothing was taken care of, and I had a hard time locating things that I used every day. For example, we never had pencils in the house. I know that sounds a little weird, but I needed pencils for homework and art projects. Everything seemed to get lost in my mom's stuff, and it was frustrating. It's not like my mom was a hoarder — she just wasn't organized and had too much stuff."

Jenna explained that she had a "good childhood," but it was really hard listening to her parents constantly argue about money. She noted, "My parents tried to keep financial matters to themselves, but it was obvious there were problems. A lot of the problems stemmed from my mom's shopping addiction. It seemed like we were always going through periods of boom or bust. We either had a little money or we were broke."

As Jenna talked about her mom and dad's financial problems, I thought about 2003, the year I got married. It was a good year, but

I lived paycheck to paycheck, with so much student loan debt that I couldn't catch up. Rather than saving money to pay it off, I would go to the mall for "shopping breaks." I could relate to Jenna's experience.

Toward the end of our conversation, Jenna expressed, "It was hard watching my parents struggle because of my mom's shopping addiction. Despite their struggles, both of my parents were there for me. They gave me their time, love, and attention. I felt secure and loved — that's all I really needed."

I interviewed Jenna in July 2011, and I keep thinking about her comment because I believe most people want time, love, and attention from their friends and family. I know that's what I want. Interestingly, by simplifying my life, I've gotten better at giving those things to others, and in turn I've gotten them back, which has made me a whole lot happier.

I've also discovered that there is no "one size fits all" approach to living simply. Concepts like minimalism, downsizing, voluntary simplicity, and even personal happiness mean different things to different people. And that's okay.

Over the past seven years, I've developed my own definition of simple living and happiness. For me that means living without a car, getting rid of debt, living in a very small house, and keeping minimal personal belongings. My aim in this book is to help you develop your own definition of simple living and happiness.

In addition, I've deliberately avoided the wider social and political aspects of these choices. For some, living simply is an active political and environmental choice; it's pursued as part of a larger belief in the need for societal change. While I agree with many of these social goals, I'm not a political pundit, and I have no interest in becoming one. My goal is to offer stories based on my experience and to provide new options for you to ponder. Does the idea of living more simply appeal to you? Does it inspire you to rethink your perspective and choices? If so, then how can you use your own unique skills and abilities to make a difference in your personal life and in your broader community? These are big questions that we each have to answer for ourselves. For myself, I put my political energy into my local volunteer work. I believe I help my community through my individual actions, as well as by being mindful of my behavior and striving to live authentically in ways that support my life purpose. In all ways, I am continually trying to simplify.

Micro-actions

Small, actionable tasks made the process of giving away my stuff, paying off my debt, and even changing careers a whole lot smoother. Instead of feeling overwhelmed, I felt empowered. At the end of each chapter, I provide a list of micro-actions to help you put these ideas into practice, so throughout the book be ready to write, talk, think, and do.

As you start, one of the first steps is to define your own version of happiness and simplicity. What does this vision look like for you? When I started to simplify my life, I asked myself two big questions: What makes me happy? And how can I simplify my life to enhance my happiness? These are great ways to begin rethinking your relationship with stuff and how you define happiness.

- **Write down *your* definition of happiness.** In a journal or just on a piece of paper, write about your own version of happiness. As you do, reflect on some of your favorite, happiest memories. Jot down where you were and who you were with, as well as sights, sounds, and smells. Capture the whole experience, and identify why these moments made you happy. For me, happiness is interwoven with strong relationships and memories that last a lifetime. What makes you happy?

- **How can you simplify your life?** Right now, write down all the ways you can think of to simplify your life. As you write, consider: What changes can you make to your daily routine that will give you more freedom and time? How will those changes make you happier?

CHAPTER 2

The Stuff You Own Owns You

We move from a teeming college dorm to an apartment
to a house, and if we're really wealthy, to an estate.
We think we're moving up,
but really we're walling ourselves off.

— Eric Weiner

I once loved to buy stuff. I loved to give it, get it, and shop for it. It turns out this is a fairly common feeling among Americans. Did you know that one of the top tourist attractions in the United States is the Mall of America? Traditional spots like the Empire State Building, Disneyworld, Mt. Rushmore, and the Grand Canyon still draw millions, but the 100-acre Mall of America is right up there in popularity, with more than forty million people visiting it each year.

Before I simplified my life, I was buying so much stuff that it was practically exploding out of my apartment. I was close to joining thousands of others who rent storage facilities every year. As of 2009, there were more than fifty thousand self-storage facilities in the United States. To put that number into context, America has fewer than thirteen thousand McDonald's and only about eleven thousand Starbucks. In 2009, the Self Storage Association said that in the previous year Americans paid more than $22 billion to store stuff in its 2.3 billion square feet of self-storage space. It is difficult to wrap one's mind around a number that large. Think of it this way — it's now possible for every single man, woman, and child in the United States to fit under a canopy of storage roofs at the same time. Perhaps even more telling is how this compares with the rest of the world. America has more than fifty thousand storage facilities, Canada about three thousand, and Australia about a thousand.

Every year on Black Friday millions of Americans get up early in the morning to line up outside of big box stores, or even camp out the night before, just to get the best deals on stuff. In November 2010, despite the Great Recession and high unemployment levels, a record number of Americans went shopping the weekend after Thanksgiving. Over 212 million people hit the malls on Black Friday, and the average person spent $365. Specifically, more than a thousand people lined up outside a Gucci outlet in California, more than seven thousand lined up outside Macy's in Manhattan, and thousands more waited in front of stores like Victoria's Secret, Best Buy, Kmart, and Walmart across the country.

That year, hundreds of people camped outside a Best Buy in California, and on Friday morning the parking lot was littered with fast-food containers and coffee cups. Store manager Nick Ramos told the *New York Times*, "It was like a shantytown out there."

There are regular reports of people being injured on Black Friday. Do you remember Jdimytai Damour, a Walmart worker who was killed in November 2008? The *New York Times* noted, "Damour had been trying to hold back a crush of shoppers pressing against the store's sliding-glass double doors. Just before the store's scheduled 5 AM opening, the doors shattered under the weight of the crowd. Mr. Damour was thrown to the floor and trampled."

In 2010, a Target shopper in Buffalo, New York, was rushed to the hospital after being trampled by a large crowd on Black Friday. The store opened at 4 AM and the crowd rushed in, completely out of control. Keith Krantz, the injured shopper, was interviewed by a local television station and said, "At that moment, I was thinking I don't want to die here on the ground. That's exactly what I thought."

Why are Americans buying so much stuff? Especially when all this stuff results in so much debt? Many people don't think they are affected by advertising, but research has shown that the average American is exposed to over three thousand ads every day and that we're deeply influenced by the messages we see. Scholars have found that shopping makes us happy. However, it's a temporary boost in happiness. That means once you've bought that new pair of shoes, new shirt, fancy leather couch, or whatever else you've had your eye on, it's not long before the happiness you get from the purchase wears off. Then it's back to the mall for more stuff.

The result? People end up literally buying their way into debt. For example, with an average credit card interest rate of 14 percent, American families pay $2,240 each year just to keep their debt from growing. Never mind actually paying it off. Like many Americans, I wound up in a constant state of indebtedness working longer and harder just to make ends meet because of my overspending on cars and apartments. As I found, the stuff you own owns you.

The Emotional Cost of Debt

The most direct way my stuff owned me was through debt. I'd buy things with my credit card — like a new vase to complement my new coffee table. I soon discovered that small purchases added up quickly, both in the price I paid and in my time. Taking care of my new stuff took effort. Then, when the monthly credit card bill arrived, I'd panic. My stomach would get upset and I'd get headaches.

Logan and I always paid our credit card bill. But we would be left with no cushion in our checking account, and the cycle would repeat each month.

Study after study has shown that debt can have a negative impact on both our physical and mental health. Dr. Sonja Lyubomirsky pointed out in her book *The How of Happiness* that "by some estimates, clinical depression is ten times more likely to torment us now that it did a century ago." She goes on to say that "15 percent of people in the United States (and 21 percent of women) will become clinically depressed at some point during their lifetimes." Of course, depression can be caused by a number of factors, but in 2007 the Institute of Psychiatry in London studied the connection between debt and depression and found that irrespective of income, debt can increase a person's chances of developing clinical depression and anxiety. It's easy to understand why. The constant stress of working to pay off credit card debt, car loans, and the mortgage can be exhausting. In addition, creeping feelings of inadequacy, despair, and shame are often associated with debt.

In July 2008, a fifty-three-year-old Massachusetts woman named Carlene Balderrama was heartbroken when her family's home was foreclosed. She hid the family's financial problems from her husband and blamed herself for mismanaging their finances. An hour and a half before her family's home was to be auctioned off she killed herself with one of her husband's hunting rifles. That same month a sixty-two-year-old New Jersey man named Emilio Saladriagas was so overwrought by all the late-payment notices he was receiving that he walked into a local Rent-A-Center, poured lighter fluid over himself, and set himself on fire. These are extreme reactions, but the stress associated with debt has a powerful effect on our well-being.

In *The Gifts of Imperfection*, Dr. Brené Brown collected over ten thousand stories about shame and vulnerability. Dr. Brown's research shows that when we don't talk about our problems, we become "desperate to numb and take the edge off, and full of so much anxiety and self-doubt that we can't act on what we *know* is best for us." For example, I know a lot about money management — I have a bachelor's degree in economics and worked in investment management — but for years I mismanaged my finances. Rather than talking about my problems, I numbed my feelings with shopping, leading to bouts of depression and arguments with my husband. As Dr. Brown points out, even if you know what's best for you, it can be hard to act on that knowledge. We live in a consumption-based culture, which has a significant impact on our behavior patterns. In his book *Branded Nation*, James Twitchel says that "much of our shared knowledge about ourselves and our culture comes to us through a commercial process of storytelling called branding" and that "ten percent of a two-year-old's nouns are brand names."

Depression and its effects are just one of the costs associated with buying stuff we can't afford. Another hidden cost is the narrowing of choices that results from working longer and harder to deal with debt. Bill McKibben points out in his book *Deep Economy* that "the more hours you work, the less satisfied you become with your life, even though you make more money." Why is that? No matter how much we make, our advertising-saturated culture tempts us to buy more and more, which perpetuates a vicious cycle of debt accumulation. In fact, in *The Overworked American*, Juliet Schor shows how people have responded to "their stressful working lives by participating in an orgy of consumer up-scaling.... Over the last thirty years, real consumption expenditures per person [have] doubled."

Participating in an "orgy" of consumer spending comes at a heavy cost — freedom of choice. Once you're caught on the work-spend treadmill, it's difficult to get off. Want to change careers? Take time off work to coach your child's soccer team? Go back to school? Volunteer at a local animal shelter? Take a sabbatical? Find an hour a day to work out? Spend more time with family and friends? If you're already in debt and working long hours to pay the bills, which keep piling up month after month, any of those things can seem like a luxury you simply can't afford.

Another cost is the harm to our communities and personal relationships. In his book *Bowling Alone*, Robert Putnam suggests that there has been a significant erosion of civic life throughout the United States, primarily because of increased working hours and suburbanization. If you're spending two hours a day commuting to and from the office, like I once did, and working longer hours to manage your debt, it's difficult to maintain quality relationships with friends and family or engage in civic life. Putnam also argues that as civic life declines, people become more likely to engage in solitary entertainment activities, like playing video games or watching television, which further erodes our communities.

It's easy to think of the cost of the things you buy only in terms of sticker price, or the up-front monetary cost of the purchase. From that point of view, if you're already thirty thousand dollars in debt, what's another couple hundred bucks? However, you keep paying for the stuff you buy: working to pay for it in the first place, dealing with the stress of debt, being locked into a job you hate, having little time to cultivate strong relationships. Living simply means ending this cycle. It's about creating more time and having less debt rather than spending all your time working, shopping, and then working more to pay for stuff you couldn't afford in the first place.

My Story: Debt, Downsizing, and Dreams

Ever since I was a kid, I wanted a house in the suburbs, with my own washing machine and dryer, a big kitchen to cook huge meals, and an extra bedroom for guests to stay in when they visited. In the spring of 2003, in my early twenties, I had a bad case of house lust, and my new husband, Logan, and I spent a lot of time talking about our mythical dream house.

I thought owning a home would be a fantastic retirement plan, and my coworkers shared this assumption. Throughout 2003 and 2004, I was part of a management-training program in the investment management industry, and all of my coworkers and supervisors said that buying a home was a worthwhile investment. To pursue our dream and this investment opportunity, Logan and I started looking in the local real estate magazines and the ads on Craigslist for a home.

One of my friends and colleagues, Janet, had recently built a beautiful custom home outside of Sacramento, California. Every time I walked into her house, I felt like I was walking into a photo shoot for *Better Homes and Gardens*. The colors and decor were stunning. I wanted what Janet had. Our little apartment seemed so small and trashy in comparison to Janet's beautiful home, with her walk-in closets, home office, and modern kitchen. I couldn't wait to become a member of the home-ownership club.

However, our plan had a problem. Once we crunched the numbers, we realized that we couldn't afford the type of home I wanted. By the time I finished up my college degrees in 2005, we had accumulated thirty thousand dollars in debt — from both student loans and car loans — and the interest on a house payment would be more than our current rent! We weren't alone. According to the Project on Student Debt, college students graduate with about twenty-four thousand dollars in student loan debt, and that doesn't include credit card debt. For example, *USA Today* reported that the average undergraduate carries over three thousand dollars in credit card debt. In 2008, "college seniors with at least one credit card graduated with an average of $4,138 in card debt, up 44 percent from 2004."

When we grasped what we were up against, I became completely depressed. I felt like a failure because we couldn't afford our dream house. I also felt angry because I had dug myself into a hole of debt even though I was working hard. Despite my job, the American Dream seemed out of reach for us.

Throughout 2003 and 2004, I'd remained largely optimistic, if not exactly excited. Working in the investment management industry wasn't what I'd always longed to do, but it was an opportunity to learn more about economics and finance, plus it allowed me to begin paying off my student loan debt. It was a job a responsible adult would accept, and my family encouraged me to continue working for the company. And yet, I spent a lot of time commuting, and sitting in a car so much was causing back problems, weight gain, and lethargy. The office environment also had a negative impact, and the work itself didn't make me feel like I was making a difference in the world. By the time I got home from work, I didn't feel like going for a walk. Instead I would sit on the couch and watch television or go shopping. It felt better to zone out and not think about my troubles.

I knew I was supposed to be happy and that I was extremely fortunate. I was married to the man of my dreams, had a terrific two-bedroom apartment in a safe neighborhood, a closet full of clothes, and a nice car. I couldn't figure out why I was so depressed. I lost my enthusiasm for life.

When I started college in 1998, my goal was to work for an organization that helped people. Making a lot of money wasn't my primary concern. I just wanted to help those who were less fortunate. Yet here I was in a place where my stuff and debt were controlling my life. I'd always considered myself smart and capable, but I started to wonder if I really was. If I was so smart, how did I get caught up in the work-spend cycle, with a huge apartment full of stuff that I didn't really want? As Will Rogers said, "Too many people spend money they haven't earned, to buy things they don't want, to impress people they don't like." That quote described me perfectly. I was living to support my stuff. As a result, I was losing my freedom, energy, and sense of self because I was less connected to my community and family.

How Did This Happen?

Research suggests that people care more deeply about what others think of them than they understand on a conscious level. In the same way, I was more obsessed with status and stuff than I realized. People want to show others that they are successful, and stuff is proof of our social status. Author Juliet Schor points to homes, clothing, and cars as "the visible triad" of stuff. These are the things we see when we meet people, and we unconsciously use stuff to assess a person's status.

In his book *Luxury Fever*, Robert Frank contends that our lust for stuff goes beyond just keeping up with the Joneses. Frank and other scholars argue that people spend money on homes, cars, and clothing not only to impress others but to reward themselves for hard work and to comfort themselves. Seven years ago, I was doing exactly what Frank talks about: buying stuff to reward myself for hard work and to impress others. My neighbors, coworkers, and friends all seemed to have the perfect life. They had dual incomes, lived in beautiful homes, owned luxury cars, and by all outward appearances were affluent and happy and had a lot of friends. I wanted those things, too.

There's nothing wrong with admiring successful people. However, research strongly suggests that upward comparisons (as in, "She makes more money than me," "He has a nicer car") can lead to feelings of low self-esteem, depression, and distress. Research demonstrates that you can't be envious and happy at the same time, and I certainly wasn't happy.

I felt like I deserved rewards for working hard. Yet, rewarding myself with stuff didn't make me happy, because I wasn't dealing with my underlying emotions. In fact, in the book *Stuff*, the authors estimate that 6 percent of US adults are addicted to shopping. That's more than 14 million people in the United States who use shopping as an outlet to help them cope with anger, stress, depression, boredom, self-critical thoughts, tension, anxiety, and loneliness. I was never clinically addicted to shopping; however, I used shopping as a way to avoid dealing with my problems.

For instance, in my early twenties I was obsessed with diamonds. My infatuation became even worse when Logan and I talked about getting married. I spent hours looking through jewelry catalogs and made secret trips to the mall trying to find the perfect engagement ring. Logan ended up buying a beautiful solitaire engagement ring for me, but I still lusted after a bigger, three-stone diamond set. A recently married friend had a bigger diamond set, and I desperately wanted something just as nice.

I convinced Logan that getting a new ring wouldn't be too expensive and told him it would make me happy. So we upgraded the solitaire diamond to a three-stone set, and we bought a diamond wedding band, too! We couldn't afford the ring, so we charged it — all four thousand dollars — on our credit card. We figured we'd pay it off later.

Writing about the diamond ring incident makes me cringe. Why did I want the ring so badly? Looking back, I think it had to do with my desire to show others that we could "afford" this kind of purchase and that I "deserved" the ring. I worked hard, so I figured it was okay to "treat" myself to a big diamond ring. However, such a huge purchase just buried us further in debt; it kept me tied to a job I wasn't happy with; and it made my fiancé feel like he couldn't afford to buy me the happiness he felt I deserved.

Now, when I look at my wedding set, I don't think about our amazing wedding day and our strong marriage. Instead, I think about how caught up in materialism I was at the time. I don't wear the ring anymore because it reminds me of the "old Tammy." Also, after several years of consideration, I've finally decided to sell the ring. The money we make from the sale will either be put in our savings account or given to charity.

Our Way Out

To get out of the work-spend cycle, Logan and I started to ask ourselves some difficult questions: What do we want out of life? How are we going to pay off our debt? What makes us happy? How can we help other people? We started talking about downsizing our lives to improve our health and financial situation. Logan was really excited about the possibility of simplifying, and I could see the wheels turning in his head. One evening, during an in-depth conversation at the kitchen table, Logan suggested, "Why don't we move into a one-bedroom apartment? If we moved closer to your office, you wouldn't have to drive or worry about taking the train. We would save a lot of money."

I carefully set my wine glass down and said, "We can't fit into a one-bedroom. We have too much stuff! Plus, where am I going to put my parents when they come to visit us. On the couch? I don't think so!"

I could see the frustration on Logan's face. He let out a big breath and calmly said, "Let's try it and see if we like living in a smaller apartment. What's the worst thing that can happen? We'll save some money, and we'll be able to get rid of some stuff in the process. Besides, we rarely have people stay in our extra bedroom. When we move into our new place we can give guests our bed, and we can camp out in the living room."

This conversation took place in late 2004, right before I left my job in the investment management industry. At this point, I had no interest in downsizing, and I'd never heard of tiny houses. I resisted the very idea of letting go of stuff and making the necessary changes to pay down our debt, but Logan kept pushing me to simplify.

What Logan said made sense, but the thought of downsizing filled me with anxiety. What would people think? I didn't want people to think we were poor (even though we really were), and I felt like downsizing was a huge step backward. I was still attached to the notion of buying a house in the suburbs. The idea of giving our stuff to charity seemed silly. We spent a lot of money acquiring all this stuff — why give it away?

All that aside, I didn't believe we could actually fit into a one-bedroom apartment. Our apartment was already overflowing with stuff. To address my concerns, Logan offered to get rid of all the shelves in his closet, his drafting table, and his ugly desk, which I had been eager to shed since the day it entered the apartment. Needless to say, the idea of getting rid of Logan's stuff was very appealing.

I felt like Logan was the one with all the extra stuff and that he was the one weighing us down. My tune changed once I started sorting through my stuff. I had a lot of excess junk, too. For instance, during high school and college I skied a lot and had accumulated a huge collection of sweaters. A quick count revealed that I had over fifty sweaters stuffed into one side of my closet. I thought to myself, what the heck — fifty sweaters? Did I really need a different sweater every day for nearly two months? I didn't even ski anymore.

As we began going through our stuff, I started to feel like we were living in a large storage unit. We didn't even use most of the things we owned. They just took up space. We had one cupboard dedicated to wedding china and another to hold all our coffee cups. We rarely used the wedding china, and really, how many coffee cups does one couple need?

Despite all the talking and purging of stuff, I still wasn't convinced we would fit in a one-bedroom apartment. Before we moved, we decided to treat our two-bedroom apartment as a one-bedroom apartment for a few months. It felt like a training regimen for a marathon. I was genuinely surprised when we actually did it! After a while that empty room started to feel like wasted space. If we weren't using it, why pay for it?

Taking Back Our Freedom

In late 2004, I left the investment management industry and went back to school for a master's degree in education. I also started volunteering regularly in 2005, and in early 2006, I began a new job as a victim advocate. During this period, we spent a lot of time giving away our stuff, and in 2006 we decided to move from a two-bedroom, 1,200-square-foot apartment to a one-bedroom, 800-square-foot apartment in Davis, California. Moving to a smaller place saved us two hundred dollars per month and gave us a whole lot of momentum to keep our lives clutter-free!

We discovered that giving away our stuff and living in a smaller space gave us more freedom, rather than less, because we weren't encumbered with so much junk. Giving our stuff to charity felt surprisingly good. Logan even sold his little blue Ford Ranger in the spring of 2004. Many of our relatives thought we were crazy and pressured us not to downsize. One relative said, "You shouldn't downsize because you have so much valuable stuff. Keep it, just in case you need it someday."

During preparation for our first move in 2006, we felt unsure about whether to hold on to certain things. When we hit these points, Logan and I encouraged each other. We would ask each other questions like: When was the last time you wore those pants? Does that make you happy? Will you actually start knitting again or not? We would make a pro/con list for the item. More importantly, we reminded each other that downsizing was about freedom: freedom from stuff and freedom from debt.

Today, Logan and I have downsized further than I ever would have imagined then, more than I would have thought possible. But it was a process; it didn't happen overnight. Initially, I read a lot about simplicity and how others let go of the excess stuff in their lives. Reading stories helped me break out of my consumerist cocoon. In the end, it took five years of shedding stuff and three moves to get where we are today, which is living in a 128-square-foot house on wheels and loving it. When we started this journey, our apartment was more than five times the size of our current dwelling. You might wonder, Why go to such extremes?

I agree with Jay Shafer's assessment of living small. Shafer runs the Tumbleweed Tiny House company, and in the movie *TINY*, he notes, "The primary asset that comes with a small house is freedom. The world gets a lot bigger when you are living small because I can afford to do a lot more things in terms of cash and time. Now the whole world is my living room."

During the 2011 Thanksgiving holiday my mom and I had an interesting conversation about stuff. In some ways she thinks our lifestyle is "extreme," particularly our participation in what's called the 100 Thing Challenge. Dave Bruno started the challenge a few years ago (and wrote a book about it). He wanted to pare down his personal possessions to less than a hundred things. One hundred sounds like a lot until you start adding up all your shirts, books, dishes, knives, forks, shoes, and so on. Ultimately, Dave's goal with the project is to get people both to live with less and to think about how consumerism affects their daily choices. At its core, the challenge is about reevaluating what you need in your life. As I explained to my mom, I have enough. I no longer feel the need to reward myself with trips to the mall.

Of course, everyone's circumstances are different. The amount of stuff you have will be different from what I have. What downsizing and simplicity mean will be different, too. The idea isn't only to count objects but to be mindful of what you bring into your life and what you use on a daily basis. For instance, I'm an avid reader and buy new books frequently. In my old life I would have kept those books. Now I donate or resell my books after I'm done reading them. It's what I call the one-in, one-out rule. Every time I buy something new, I donate something to charity.

You don't have to live in a tiny apartment or with very few possessions to embrace simplicity. Instead, figure out how you can incorporate the principles of simplicity into your life. For instance, if you want to "reward" yourself for working hard, don't buy more things; spend money on experiences or donate your extra cash to a cause you believe in.

I struggled with this concept for years. It wasn't until I read the classic book *Your Money or Your Life* by Joe Dominguez and Vicki Robin that I started to rethink how I spent my money, or, as the authors call it, "life energy." Their idea is that when you spend money on a product, you trade a piece of your time for it. Before you purchase any product, consider how much time you'll have to spend working to pay for it.

Rather than cluttering up your home, stealing your time, and draining your wallet, the stuff in your life should serve a purpose and make you happy. If that isn't the case, then your stuff owns you.

Micro-actions

Below are a few micro-actions that helped me let go of stuff. I hope they help you, too!

- **Stay away from the mall.** I know this sounds obvious, but it's harder than it seems, especially if you enjoy shopping. Staying away from the mall was a key action for me. When I stopped going shopping, I stopped bringing home stuff I didn't need or really want. If I had to go to the mall, I made a list of the things I needed and stuck to the list.
- **Sort through your stuff, slowly.** If you want to declutter your home, it's important to take small steps every day.

I'd recommend starting with one room and then creating piles of stuff you want to keep and other items you'd like to donate. For example, you could donate ten items a week to the charity of your choice. This process takes time. However, it's fruitful. Undertaking a gradual transition will help you start a new routine, and it's more likely to outlast quick lifestyle fixes.

- **Try the 100 Thing Challenge.** The 100 Thing Challenge helped me figure out what I really needed in my life. No matter how much stuff you have, the challenge will force you to inventory your possessions and examine your buying patterns. The biggest challenge associated with this project is deciding what to count and what not to count. If you opt to take on this challenge, remember it's your challenge and you can create your own rules. For instance, Dave Bruno, the guy who started the challenge, counted his library as one thing! And that's totally cool. The idea is to adapt the challenge to fit your life and needs.
- **Write down an extensive list of your fears.** For example, when I started downsizing, I was scared of what people would think of us. I didn't want to be cast out of my social group because I didn't have a car, a traditional house, or a lot of stuff. This fear never came true. At first friends and family weren't sure what to think of my decision, but after a lot of conversations, they supported me.
- **Find a support network.** Simplifying is a process. Don't be hard on yourself if you are having a hard time paring down. Have patience and find a support network to hold you accountable. Blogging about my journey helped me stick to my goals because I was accountable to a whole group of readers. They were rooting for me, and I wanted to succeed! Consider starting a blog and publicly document your journey.

PART 2

Finding Happiness through Simple Living

CHAPTER 3

Changing Your Relationship with Stuff

I believe examining the hidden impacts of all the Stuff in our lives... is the first step toward changing things.

— Annie Leonard

As I sat in my Economics 101 class, I fidgeted in my chair and resisted the urge to run around the classroom. My professor was talking about international trade in a monotone voice, making it hard to focus. Despite his lack of enthusiasm, my curiosity was piqued when he mentioned gross domestic product (GDP). He defined GDP as "the metric we use to measure economic growth," which as Annie Leonard, author of *The Story of Stuff*, puts it, simply means more of everything: "More stuff. More money. Just like it sounds, growth means getting bigger."

Even though my Econ 101 professor lacked enthusiasm, the topics he discussed challenged me and made me thirsty for more information. I started taking additional economics classes for fun, and eventually, I declared my major in economics and earned my degree in the subject. As I delved deeper, I noticed a theme. My professors talked a lot about the importance of economic growth, but they spent very little time talking about well-being — the "dismal profession" didn't seem very concerned with happiness. However, the economics department possessed one outlier.

One of my favorite teachers, Professor Michael Perelman, encouraged his students to question "normal" policy decisions. He focused on topics like happiness and consumerism, and he argued that an economic model based on continuous growth wasn't good policy. Why? Professor Perelman noted that GDP leaves out some really important metrics.

Robert Kennedy explained the problem beautifully. He said GDP doesn't register "the health of our children, the quality of their education, or the joy of their play. It does not include the beauty of our poetry or the strength of our marriages; the intelligence of our public debate or the integrity of our public officials. It measures neither our wit nor our courage; neither our wisdom nor our learning; neither our compassion nor our devotion to our country; it measures everything, in short, except that which makes life worthwhile."

So what does GDP measure? The economic growth in productivity, consumption, services, and trade that results from things like the war in Iraq, oil spills, the destruction of forests, the cost of a nuclear warhead, and all the stuff we buy at the mall.

This leads to a very big question: What's the point of measuring growth if we're unhappy? In *The End of Growth*, Richard Heinberg writes, "The subject of happiness was mostly avoided by economists for lack of good ways to measure it; however, in recent years, 'happiness economists' have found ways to combine subjective surveys with objective data (on lifespan, income, and education) to yield data with consistent patterns, making a national happiness index a practical reality."

Richard Heinberg goes on to explain that right before the 2008 financial crisis, US households were "spending almost 19 percent of their disposable income on servicing their debt. Total outstanding household debt also peaked in 2008 just before the financial crisis at $14 trillion. To put this in perspective, the entire US economy was worth $14.3 trillion that same year." No wonder we're seeing higher levels of stress, depression, anxiety, and unhappiness. It's not shocking when you find out that the average household spends about 20 percent of its disposable income paying off debt.

As Tim Kasser said, "Sages from almost every religious and philosophical background have similarly insisted that focusing on material possession and social renown detracts from what is meaningful about life." Yet cultural messages tell people that "bigger is better" and that the consumption of stuff will make us feel successful and powerful. As a result, we leverage ourselves to the maximum. I did, and I see friends and family members doing the same thing: maxing out their credit cards, taking out second mortgages and high-interest loans for boats, cars, homes, and so on. Logan and I first started to question our lifestyle soon after we got married in 2003. But it wasn't until I took a trip to Chiapas, Mexico, in 2005, that my mindset shifted, and I saw the link between my personal actions and the economics of happiness discussed in my economics courses.

A New Direction

One year before moving to a new, smaller apartment, I decided to quit my job in the investment management industry. Logan and I were in the midst of our first discussions about downsizing and simplifying our lives, but I already knew that one key to improving my personal happiness was to change careers and find more meaningful work. As part of that, in early 2005 I started volunteering with the Mexico Solidarity Network (MSN) — an organization that advocates for democracy, economic justice, and humans rights on both sides of the US-Mexico border. Their main office was in Chicago, but they had volunteers throughout the United States, and I kept in touch with my supervisor via email and the phone.

As a volunteer I sold artisan goods produced by the Zapatistas, an indigenous community in Chiapas, Mexico. We worked with a women's artisan collective, called Women for Dignity, which produced handmade goods like bracelets, blouses, bags, pillowcase covers, and small quilts. The Zapatistas have been called many things, from communists to modern-day heroes, depending on your perspective and political ideology. Since 1994, the Zapatistas have been fighting for control of their local resources, especially their land, and they have developed partnerships with organizations like MSN to support their communities.

Every Saturday morning, I would crawl out of bed, make coffee, and pack up my Honda station wagon with a suitcase filled with beautiful artisan goods. Then I'd head over to the farmer's market and set up my small folding table to sell things like coffee, handmade clothes and jewelry, books, and other crafts. The money from my sales was sent back to the Zapatistas and used for a variety of community programs, including education and health care.

Logan supported my volunteer activities and frequently helped me sell artisan goods at the farmer's market. Then one day I told him I wanted to visit Mexico.

"You want to go where?!" Logan exclaimed.

"To Chiapas. It's the southernmost state in Mexico. I just got an email from a staff member at Mexico Solidarity Network, and she said they will be leading a delegation to Oventic, one of the Zapatista communities. It's close to San Cristobal de las Casas. I think this trip would be a perfect complement to the volunteer work I've been doing with them."

Logan sighed heavily and said, "I don't know, Tammy. I know you're really interested in alternative economies, and I'm on board with most of the philosophies promoted by the Zapatistas, but Chiapas is a highly militarized state. I don't think it's safe to travel down there. Plus, we still have so much student loan debt. Don't you think we should pay that off before we spend money on a big trip?"

I rolled my eyes and said, "Whatever. I don't care about the debt. We'll always be in debt, so we might as well go. This is a once-in-a-lifetime opportunity, and I don't think it's as dangerous as you think. Besides, I've already made my decision. I'm going, with or without you."

Despite our arguments about the trip, I had a sneaking suspicion he'd come with me. I was right. I distinctly remember him telling me, "You're so stubborn sometimes. I'm nervous about the trip, but I'd be even more nervous and worried if I stayed at home. So I might as well go with you."

If we were being practical, we should have stayed home and focused on downsizing our stuff and debt. Yet Logan told me that he'd never seen me save for anything before. The more I learned about the Zapatistas, the more I started rethinking my relationship with stuff, happiness, and how I could use my skills to make a difference in the world.

Another World

When we flew into Mexico City, I finally realized what Logan meant when he said Mexico was a highly militarized state — we weren't even in Chiapas, and police officers were strolling through the airport with machine guns. I'd traveled outside of the United States as a kid, but not as an adult. Seeing military weapons displayed so openly was shocking.

As we were waiting for our flight to leave Mexico City, we met some of the other volunteers and started chatting. Soon we boarded the flight, and before we knew it we had landed in Tuxtla Gutiérrez, Mexico. Jennifer, one of the staff members at MSN, said that a cab would pick us up at the airport. We waited for at least an hour, but the taxi never appeared. Emilio, a fellow intern who spoke fluent Spanish, told us not to worry. He said we could catch a bus to San Cristobal and meet the rest of the volunteers; we just needed a ride from the airport to the bus station.

Emilio explained our situation to an older gentleman, who offered to take us to the city center for a small fee. The guy wove through other cars on the road like a race car driver, and I thought I was going to die. To distract myself, I focused on the warm, fresh air hitting my face. As we zoomed through the city, I saw dusty shacks that people called home and children as young as five selling candy and crafts on the street.

Taking all this in made me want to cry because I realized how selfish I had been in the past. As a white, middle-class, privileged American woman, I had spent years chasing after stuff and constantly thirsting for more. I was so concerned about my own happiness that I had failed to notice how many people in the world suffer because they don't have enough.

The car suddenly came to a halt and jolted me out of my thoughts. It was time to get on the bus. The bus was sweltering, and tiny beads of sweat ran down my forehead and back, but the countryside was beautiful. The bus slowly made its way around the twists and turns of the mountain road. The higher we climbed, the steeper the terrain became. As the bus crawled up, we passed all kinds of little farms. I was amazed at how creative the farmers were; many of them had planted rows of corn on steep hillsides, and cows stood at awkward angles munching on weeds.

By the time we rolled into San Cristobal, I was increasingly thankful for Emilio. Logan and I didn't know much Spanish, and without Emilio we never would have made it. We knocked on the door, and Jennifer appeared. She said, "I was starting to get worried about you guys. Was the cab late?"

Emilio looked confused and said, "The cab driver never picked us up. We hitched a ride into town and then took the bus."

"Oh no! I paid the cab driver before he left San Cristobal. He must have taken off with the cash. I'm so sorry! I'm glad you guys made it safe and sound. Come in!"

We got settled in, regrouped, and talked about the agenda for the next week. The plan was to stay in San Cristobal for the next few days, attend a few lectures, and then go to the Zapatista village, Oventic. On our first night in San Cristobal, we spent our time walking, exploring, and people watching. The city was awe inspiring, full of original, well-maintained Spanish architecture. The homes had red-tiled roofs, the streets were lined with cobblestones, and many of the second-story apartments and hotels had iron balconies lined with flowers.

As the trip progressed, I realized that this was the first time I'd ever lived out of a backpack. Granted, the trip was only a few weeks long, but it opened my eyes to a new world and a new way of life. I realized how easily I could pare down my personal belongings. I didn't need as much as I thought, and I was thankful that I'd only brought a backpack. Before the trip, Logan and I had talked extensively about what to bring. When I showed Logan the duffle bag I wanted to take, he looked at me and said, "You can't bring that!"

I was perplexed. "Why not?"

"Honey, we're going to be walking all over the place. Do you really want to bring a huge bag that you'll have to lug around?"

Heeding his advice, I decided to splurge and buy a backpack, spending a little bit more than I wanted. However, it was worth the investment. Now, in addition to my bike, computer, and camera, my backpack is one of my favorite belongings. A lot of the other volunteers packed heavily. Our friend Rosalie was forced to lug her huge suitcase over the cobblestone streets; the bag's wheels weren't much help in this situation. Other volunteers with big pieces of luggage complained because they felt like "typical Americans," carrying around bags of useless stuff.

When we finally visited Oventic, I wasn't sure what to expect. Listening to the Zapatistas talk about their struggles for basic rights, like access to their land, health care, and education, was sobering. Yet despite their difficult circumstances, they seemed happy, even joyous. I don't want to romanticize their struggles, but they had a strong connection to their community that I envied. At the time, this was something I wanted.

In Chiapas, I clearly saw my own privileged economic status. The Zapatistas had none of the "necessities" that filled my life, including our luxury apartment, cars, fancy clothes, and television. If the Zapatistas could live simply, paint beautiful murals, and be happy even in the midst of their political and military struggles with the government, something inside me had to change.

Returning Home

Traveling to Chiapas was a privilege. Not everyone has the option of flying to Mexico just to "rethink" their worldview. If I hadn't visited the Zapatistas, I don't think I would have considered living simply or listened to Logan about downsizing. The trip was a fundamental stepping-stone toward a better life, a life focused on my health, happiness, and service to my community, not the accumulation of stuff.

Of course, you don't need to travel the globe to rethink your worldview, either. All it takes is a commitment to becoming the change you want to see in the world. It might sound cheesy, but it's the only way to make an impact. From personal experience, I've found that shifting my focus away from stuff and toward community has changed my perception of the world. When I visited the Zapatistas, I met a group of people who had a sense of place, of belonging, and who believed deeply in creating powerful, local economies. They didn't need anything more than what they had to do this.

The Zapatista communities reminded me of Alan Durning's vision of living well. A quote by Durning in a Worldwatch Institute report stuck with me. He noted, "Accepting and living by sufficiency rather than excess offers a return to what is, culturally speaking, the human home: to the ancient order of family, community, good work, and the good life; to a reverence for skill, creativity, and creation; to a daily cadence slow enough to let us watch the sunset and stroll by the water's edge; to communities worth spending a lifetime in; and to local places pregnant with the memories of generations."

Micro-actions

As you begin to rethink your relationship to stuff, consider adding these activities to your to-do list.

- **When you travel, pack less.** Rather than bringing along a suitcase loaded with stuff on your next weekend or week-long adventure, challenge yourself and only bring a backpack. Take note of how the experience makes you feel and what comes up for you in the process. This might sound a little hokey, but it works.
- **Wait thirty days before buying stuff.** Today, if I decide to buy anything new, I wait for thirty days (sometimes longer). Incorporating a waiting period into my routine has helped me avoid impulse purchases and truly think about my needs versus my wants. For instance, I recently purchased

an iPhone. I wanted to run out and buy one when they were released in 2007. But I waited until 2012!

- **Adopt the "one-in, one-out" rule.** In addition to waiting thirty days before buying anything new, I'm a fan of the one-in, one-out rule. Every time I buy something new, I give something to charity. Whether I buy a new book, sweater, or shirt, I always give something else away.

CHAPTER 4

The Power of Debt

To change one's life, start immediately,
do it flamboyantly, no exceptions.

— William James

As I sat in the car and stared at the bumper in front of me, I wanted to scream. I was frustrated, literally stuck. My body and mind felt stiff and heavy, like a giant brick. I was killing myself with too much sitting, too much drinking, too much stress, and way too much debt. For over a year I'd been sitting in the same traffic jam, which, just like my debt, was preventing me from getting where I wanted to go.

I couldn't help but laugh at the irony of my situation. I was working in the investment management industry, which preached the importance of long-term investments, creating an emergency savings fund, paying off credit card balances, and being aware of outstanding expenses. I wasn't following any of this basic advice. Our financial life resembled a cluttered closet. We had too many accounts and too many credit cards. Everything was out of place and unorganized.

Logan and I both felt overwhelmed and stressed out. The quality of our lives was deteriorating. It was 2004 and I didn't see any way out. The three-thousand-pound straw that eventually broke the camel's back — and that finally forced us to declare war on our debt — was our decision to buy a new car.

Our Brand-New Car

It was summertime in Davis, California, and the air was hot and dry, the heat suffocating. The temperature was 102 degrees, and our air conditioner was broken. Rather than staying in the sweltering apartment, Logan and I decided to brave the outdoor weather and have a picnic. If we were lucky, a breeze might come through the yard and cool us off.

Our apartment complex had a number of grassy areas with picnic tables and benches, but we set up on the lawn. I spread out a giant quilt (recently purchased at a fundraiser) and laid out our feast. We filled our bellies with fresh bread, strawberries, blueberries, apples, cheese, and a few cookies. Stuffed, we lay back on the blanket to admire the clear blue sky. The heat aside, it was a perfect Saturday afternoon.

Then I brought up the subject of buying a new car, and our mood quickly shifted. We already had two cars, but the one I drove was old and unreliable and I wanted to replace it. However, a new car would add to our big pile of debt. Logan and I started bickering. I said, "We might as well purchase a new car. We'll be in debt for the rest of our lives anyway. There is no way I'll ever pay off my student loans. Besides, everyone is telling us that we need a new car. Even my dad said it's something we should consider!"

Logan rolled his eyes and said, "That's a horrible reason to buy a new car."

"But what about my job? I need a reliable car for work."

"I don't know, Tammy. Let's run the numbers and see what we come up with."

That evening we compared the cost of buying a new car with that of keeping the old one, and we concluded that it would be less expensive to buy a new car than to keep the old one running. The old car had already gone through two transmissions, the air conditioner was broken, and a variety of other problems kept cropping up. These things took our time and energy, in addition to our money. Plus, the old car had once broken down on the freeway, leaving me on the roadside on a sweltering summer day waiting for a tow truck. I simply didn't trust the old car anymore, and buying a new car seemed to make sense. At least, that's how we justified the expense.

Rather than continuing to argue about expenses we decided to try something new. To gain a sense of control over our debt, we started to write down our goals. Unwittingly, we were engaging in a reflective activity called "Best Possible Selves," where you keep a journal about future goals. According to researchers, writing down goals can help you visualize the future you see yourself living. Writing down our goals was the beginning of the visualization process that led to our new lives. We realized it would be a whole lot easier to pursue our dreams without being saddled with debt. For example, I dreamed of leaving my day job, but until our debt was paid off, that dream would not become a reality.

Part of the process of developing our plan to pay off our debt entailed listing all of our expenses. When we closely examined our budget and spending patterns, we realized our biggest expense, other than rent, was our cars. The numbers were shocking! Car payments, interest, insurance, gas, and maintenance added up to a total cost of ten thousand dollars per year. We were just above the national average. The auto club AAA estimates that the average American spends about nine thousand dollars annually, or 20 percent of his or her total income, on car-related expenses.

Letting go of our cars was the hardest part of downsizing, and we did it in stages. First, Logan sold his old Ford Ranger in late 2004. Then, in 2006, I sold my old Honda station wagon, and we purchased a blue Honda Fit. Ironically, one result of buying our new car was coming to the decision that, to really change our lives and realize our dreams, we needed to go car-free.

Pedaling toward Financial Freedom

I had expected the transition toward a car-lite lifestyle to be difficult, but it wasn't so bad. Logan cycled to school, and I became jealous seeing how much fun he was having. It prompted me to drive less. During 2006 and early 2007, when we still lived in Davis, I started commuting via Amtrak's Capitol Corridor train to downtown Sacramento and then walking the final mile to my office. The commute took fifteen minutes longer, but it was a great way to start the day. I got a little bit of exercise, and I was saving two hundred dollars in parking fees every month! Rather than being stuck in traffic, I was walking and biking, which made me feel happier and more at ease, and it boosted my self-esteem. Studies back up my experience. Getting enough exercise reduces stress and makes you a whole lot happier.

In fact, we were driving so little that I was calling AAA frequently to get the car jump-started. Since it was still relatively new, I couldn't figure out why it wouldn't start in the mornings. At the local dealership, a mechanic explained that I was no longer driving the car enough to charge the battery. Apparently, I needed to get out on the highway more.

Our next step was becoming clear. In 2007 we moved to Sacramento, sold the Honda Fit, and transitioned to a car-free lifestyle. For everyday needs, Logan and I bicycled or used public transportation. Pedaling toward financial freedom would never have crossed my mind during college or when I first started working in the investment management industry. I always considered car ownership to be a necessity. I "needed" a car to get to and from work. I never imagined that I'd be picking up my groceries on my bike, going camping on my bike, and having fun without an internal combustion engine.

Even though today we still don't own a car, we do rent vehicles for long trips. For example, we're members of Zipcar — a car-sharing service. Now, for the privilege of driving, we spend on average about $1,500 a year on Zipcar rentals (which includes a monthly fee and rental fees). Going car-free isn't an option for everyone, but reducing one's car use (and financial burden) by owning fewer cars or sharing a vehicle is worth considering.

Interestingly, the idea of sharing is gaining traction in the business world. I asked Lisa Gansky, author of *The Mesh: Why the Future of Business Is Sharing*, about why sharing is so important. She remarked, "Peer-to-peer transportation like RelayRides, GetAround, and Spride in the US, and WhipCar in the UK, use technology to allow you to gain access to and rent your neighbor's vehicle when they're not using it. This provides more utility for the community, as the number of cars parked and sitting around decreases. Secondly, sharing cars creates a type of bond between the owner and the borrower, and third, people using these early services are generating additional income of about $300 to $750 per month." In addition to the services Gansky mentioned, Hertz is introducing their own car-sharing service to compete with Zipcar and Carshare.

Gansky went on to say, "This same strategy applies to homes, offices, shops, land, rooftops, tools, and high fashion.... The appeal of a less-materialistic lifestyle is thrust forward when we can gain access to goods and services only when we want and need them. We are aligning the value we place on things with the cost of using them.

This balance will naturally create a less-materialistic lifestyle than the highly acquisitive one we are still recovering from."

Making the decision to structure our lives around biking and alternative forms of transportation has changed our lives for the better. Yet it's a step-by-step process. It begins with assessing your situation and finding creative, powerful ways to reduce your outstanding bills. If you have debt, don't be hard on yourself. You're not alone. As Logan and I were taking our own small baby steps, I started reading blogs focused on simple living. I found a blog called Zen Habits by Leo Babauta, who was also trying to pay off debt, declutter, and change careers. His story helped me write a new one.

Leo Babauta: The Debt Snowball Method

Leo told me that 2005 was one of the worst years of his life. Leo said, "I was living paycheck to paycheck at that time, and I was spending way more than I was making." Leo was juggling both little debts and big debts: medical bills, car payments, and credit card debt. Creditors would call his house asking for payments, and he could never seem to catch up. He said, "The bills were piling up, and we had little kids to feed. It wasn't a happy time in my life. One of my worst moments was when I didn't have any money in the bank and we needed food. So I had to raid my kids' piggy bank. Of course, I paid them back, but it was a horrible feeling. I know people suffer more than that, but it was a really bad time for me."

I asked Leo how he managed to get out of debt. He explained, "When I first started to simplify my life, I quit smoking, but tackling debt happened around the same time. When I wrote down my expenses and income, it was obvious that my income wasn't enough. So we began by writing down all our debts. It was a scary but necessary step. I had to stop the [financial] bleeding." Leo and his wife began tracking their expenses and cutting out the excess. They stopped eating out; they stopped buying lattes and instead made coffee at home. They cut the cable TV and subscription services. All of these small actions were a step in the right direction that made big impacts down the road.

Leo and his wife also ditched one of their two cars. This was much harder than going without cable. The Babautas have six kids, and living with one less car was initially inconvenient, but it became easier as they got used to the new routine. Eventually, they decided to get rid of their other car, and now Leo and his family are car-free! Leo said, "Looking back it seems really obvious, but when you're in the middle of it, that's just how your life is and it seems normal."

The Babautas were able to go car-free because they live in San Francisco, and so they are able to take advantage of the city's public transportation system. In comparison, the suburbs are not as transit-friendly or walkable, and this comes at a cost. According to a 2011 article in *The Atlantic* magazine, "Families living in auto-dependent neighborhoods spend significantly more money on transportation, with fewer dollars available for health care, food, and other family expenses."

I asked Leo how the shift from materialism to simplicity affected their kids. Leo discovered that "simplifying and finding ways to be frugal was an amazing way to reconnect with our family. Even if I wasn't in debt, I would do this all over again. All the things we did with our family were free and frugal."

Instead of spending time at the mall, Leo and his family started playing with the kids outside and getting active. They played kickball and soccer in the backyard and spent time reading together and playing board games. Leo noted, "You will always spend if you're at the mall. It's a place designed to make you spend."

Leo said that simplifying with kids is "definitely more of a challenge, not 'impossible.' If you believe it's impossible, it certainly is. I have six kids and have simplified a great deal — we have regular decluttering sessions with them and have conversations with them about owning too much stuff and what they really use and need."

For Leo, simplifying his life was a slow process that was about improving the quality of his family's life as much as about spending less money. He remarked, "It's an ongoing conversation with your kids, not something that can change overnight. I also try to lead by example and show them that you don't need a lot of stuff to be happy. Most importantly, you shouldn't overschedule your kids' lives — they don't need classes and sports and clubs and other activities to keep them busy all the time. It's better to have lots of unstructured time so they can play and be imaginative and have some downtime. Family time is important to me, too — simplify your commitments, so that you can have some unstructured, unplugged family time."

How did Leo simplify his life and get out of debt? In addition to tracking expenses and cutting back, Leo used the "debt snowball method." He learned about this approach from Dave Ramsey, an author and radio show host. The debt snowball method is fairly simple. Basically, you pay off one debt at a time, starting with small debts and slowly working your way up to larger ones. As each debt got paid, the forward momentum gave Leo and his family hope and tangible steps to work toward.

Leo also increased his income by doing freelance work. When his blog started making money, he was able to pay off his debt even faster. J. D. Roth of Get Rich Slowly, a blog that focuses on "sensible personal finance," was one of Leo's biggest inspirations. Leo noted, "If you're trying to pay off your debt, connect with one or two bloggers online who are going through the same struggles. J. D.'s blog had commonsense advice that I needed to hear. By sharing my own story on Zen Habits, I was able to pay back what J. D. gave to me." Leo encourages people to share their story by blogging, and I agree.

Blogging your journey is really helpful because it motivates you and helps others, and it is one way to reflect on your life choices.

As Leo noted, "Getting out of debt and simplifying are two sides of the same coin. Getting out of debt happened because of simplicity. Living simply has helped me stay out of debt. Simplicity is an amazing way of life because you focus on the things that matter most, and you realize that all the other stuff — like the big house, a new car, and the latest clothes — don't matter. Buying things is just one way to impress other people, and it has a huge cost in terms of time, money, and stress. These days I live a life where I do things that I'm most passionate about, which is writing, spending time with my wife and kids, and reading. I'm rich in time and rich in relationships. Since I have more time, my relationships are much better. I'm much happier now."

Micro-actions

Using the tips and strategies in this chapter, Logan and I paid off thirty thousand dollars in debt and saved up for the little house we live in now. Along the way I became a whole lot happier. Consider incorporating the following tips into your own life, using the ones that work and discarding the ones that don't. As Mark Twain once said, "Twenty years from now you will be more disappointed by the things that you didn't do than by the ones you do. So throw off the bowlines. Sail away from the safe harbor. Catch the trade winds in your sails. Explore. Dream. Discover."

- **Use your credit cards sparingly or cut them up.** Trim your credit cards to only one or two, and don't use them for everyday expenses. Their convenience can be misleading, so if you have to use a credit card make sure you are being mindful about your spending. For instance, it's hard to rent a car without a credit card.

- **Eliminate nonessential spending.** Trimming back your large expenses is the quickest way to pay off your debt, but often the hardest. However, eliminating smaller, nonessential spending is just as important and helpful. Maybe you can't live without a car, but you can save in a dozen smaller ways: for instance, cut back on eating out, shopping for clothing, and subscription-based services. Rethink the way you do things: instead of watching cable and drinking in bars, take walks, check out books from the library, and cook meals at home for friends.
- **Create a spending plan.** Know what your expenses are and how you will pay for them each month. Creating a spending plan reduces stress and increases happiness; at a minimum, you know that specific sacrifices are in service of a larger goal, getting your finances under control. Start by looking at your core expenses and create a spending plan around those things. Make sure you cover housing costs, food, and utilities, then you know what else you can afford (or save) each month. Don't forget to consider outliers, or expenses that only come up once a year or so. Some months are more expensive than others. For instance, Christmas usually means traveling to see family, so we make it a point to save for that cost throughout the year.
- **Examine your attitude about money.** People have different attitudes about money, debt, and income, and these can influence how easy, or hard, it is to live simply and debt-free. What are your guiding principles around money? What role does money play in your life? Does your level of income define you as a person and how you envision success?
- **Increase your income.** Obviously, if your income isn't keeping up with your expenses, one solution is to increase your income. Explore ways to make a little extra.

- **Establish an emergency fund.** Consider putting a small amount of money into a savings account every month. It's a great insurance policy. For example, this "insurance" helps me worry less, since now, whenever an unexpected bill comes up, I know we can pay it rather than charging it to our credit card.
- **Give yourself a reward.** Paying off your debt can be a long process, so it's important to give yourself rewards along the way, like going for a bike ride, taking a walk, or buying small treats like a coffee. Establish milestones and specific rewards for reaching them.

CHAPTER 5

Sell What You Can, Give the Rest Away

I am still letting go of my stuff and feel lighter every day.

— Courtney Carver

Today, I live in a tiny house on wheels that's only 128 square feet. Tape off that space in your own apartment or house and imagine living in it, much less fitting all your possessions into it. When Logan and I first began discussing moving into a tiny house in 2007, I didn't know if I could do it.

But I did. I had to shed a lot of stuff along the way, and I know how difficult it is to give up material possessions. Even today, a little voice will pop up in my head and say, "Don't give that away! You might need it someday!" The problem is, "someday" may never come, and in the meantime all your stuff takes away from today.

A big part of simplifying your life is simplifying your stuff. Think about how much of your life is dedicated to acquiring and managing things. Consider how much time you spend cleaning and organizing your stuff. Even if you only spend about 10 hours a week dealing with your stuff, that's 520 hours each year. How could you use that time instead? Maybe volunteering? Or spending more time with loved ones? Or focusing on your passions? As you shed your excess stuff, you'll feel lighter, more free. You'll have more time to dedicate to the people and activities in your life that really make you happy. I resisted letting go of stuff when we started this process in 2005, but I fell in love with decluttering because it made me so happy. Decluttering makes you feel good, whether you live in a tiny house or not.

Food Fight

As we walked toward the Zipcar, the rain turned into a drizzle and the sun started peeking through the clouds. The sun was so bright that we had to squint to see the sidewalk as we turned along Northwest 23rd Avenue in Portland, Oregon, which was crowded with people bustling in and out of high-end stores like the Pottery Barn and Williams & Sonoma. The street is known as "Trendy Third" because it's lined with dozens of boutique shops and great restaurants. When we were newlyweds, Logan and I would have stopped to window-shop and buy things for our (future) house. Not now. By 2011 Logan and I were consumed with getting rid of stuff and with the prospect of building a house far smaller than the apartment we lived in.

We were going to meet Michelle, a friend of a friend who had recently built a little house and lived on the outskirts of Portland. She lived there with her orange tabby cat, George; her dog, Alley; and her boyfriend. She'd offered to give us a tour over tea as well as plenty of advice about designing, building, and living in our own little house.

We had considered biking. However, Michelle's house was a twenty-mile ride from our apartment, and I was just getting over the flu. We'd become members of the car-sharing service Zipcar for just this sort of situation; the car we were picking up was a red Prius, which was nicknamed Paine. Zipcar names its cars, which is a hilarious touch. Soon, in Paine, we left Trendy Third and Portland itself and were transported into a whole new world of farms, narrow winding roads, and big old houses. In the summer, some of these "you-pick" farms allow you to pick (for a fee) your own strawberries, raspberries, blueberries, blackberries, marionberries, tree-ripened peaches, sweet corn, pears, nectarines, tomatoes, and peppers.

The rural setting was so serene and quiet, and the beaming sun made the beautiful farmland sparkle from the recent rainfall. Nonetheless, I couldn't help thinking that, if we moved here, it would be a long commute into downtown Portland.

As we pulled into Michelle's driveway, I looked at the house in complete awe. The little dwelling had rough-hewn cedar siding, a metal roof, and even a tiny red door! Then I noticed our Zipcar was probably as long as Michelle's house, and I started laughing.

As I sat enthralled with the cuteness of the house, George, Michelle's cat, jumped onto the hood of the car and meowed. I think that's the best greeting I've ever received. Michelle apologized for George's behavior, and we chatted outside for a while.

Michelle invited us in. We settled into her window nook as she made tea. We were highly amused to watch as George climbed up the loft ladder and settled in for his afternoon nap. While George slept, we had a great conversation about happiness, family, acceptance, and designing and living in such a little house. Michelle was welcoming, open, and honest, and we connected immediately. She told us that she decided to sell most of her belongings, rent out her 2,000-square-foot house, and build her very tiny house on wheels because she wanted more time to focus on her passion, which is teaching (not cleaning). She said the decluttering process wasn't as hard as she thought, and she felt happier now.

Michelle was very inspiring, and when our visit was over and we were driving back to Portland, I became animated and happy as Logan and I discussed the possibility of building our own little house. However, the familiar tug of anxiety soon pulled at my thoughts: What about our stuff? It would never fit in such a little house. I got increasingly anxious as I catalogued all our possessions, and soon Logan and I got into a heated discussion about bulk food storage.

You see, about four years before, when we lived in Davis, California, Logan started buying food in bulk. He reasoned that buying food in bulk is less expensive and that it's good to have extra food on hand if there is a natural disaster. He told me that FEMA advises people to be prepared to live without assistance for at least seventy-two hours, but post–Hurricane Katrina, many experts say to prepare for up to one to two weeks.

I was on board with the idea of buying bulk food until he told me he thought that we should have a six-month supply. An Idaho-based company could send prefilled buckets of food. Not only did the idea sound a little crazy and extreme, but I wasn't thrilled with the idea of huge buckets of grain and rice taking up so much space and adding to our apartment's physical clutter. But I acquiesced because I wanted to be supportive.

On August 11, 2007, Logan placed an order with Survival Acres, and about a month later, twelve six-gallon white buckets were delivered to our apartment. We had to reassure our landlord that we weren't crazy — that the buckets contained food and not supplies for some secret marijuana-growing operation. Thankfully, the buckets fit neatly into our huge closet, and I didn't think of them again. At least not until we moved from Davis to Sacramento. The buckets came with us even as our living space shrank to a 400-square-foot apartment. Soon after the move, I convinced Logan that we should store some of the buckets at his parents' place.

As a result, we pared our food storage down from twelve to six buckets, yet those six buckets had to come with us on our move to Portland, and they now seemed emblematic of a larger problem I had trouble articulating.

On the car ride back from Michelle's house, Logan said, "I don't understand why you hate the buckets so much. Having the buckets in the house makes me feel secure. If a disaster strikes, we'll be able to eat for a while. I thought you were on board with the idea?"

I looked out the window and said, "I thought so, too. I'm not sure why I'm so annoyed by the buckets. For me it boils down to a few things. First of all, the buckets take up a lot of space. Second, I want to eat the food in the buckets. We're only eating some of the bulk food. Half of it just sits in the closet. We don't have a lot of stuff, but it seems like we're holding on to an unnecessary amount of food."

Our discussion escalated into a full-fledged fight; I called Logan a squirrel, and in turn, he said I was being irresponsible. Over the next few weeks, Logan and I kept talking about the food buckets, and I came to realize that my anxiety over food storage was rooted in fear. I wanted to build a little house, but I was scared that we wouldn't be able to fit. Looking back, fights like this were almost inevitable, and they forced us to communicate clearly about our feelings. Our heated discussions over food storage were repeated in different ways whenever it came time to pare down other physical belongings — old clothing, books, and other clutter. We were always holding on to stuff for reasons that felt important, and letting those reasons go, or seeing them differently, was also part of the decluttering process.

In the end, we decided to donate most of the bulk food we weren't eating and to only keep the types of food that we consistently ate every week, like rice, quinoa, and wheat for bread and cookies. Today, we still maintain an emergency food storage, but it's pared down to a two-month supply that fits in the space we have.

Live Small, Think Big, and Avoid Storables

As I cleared off our bookshelf, a series of rapid-fire questions came out of my mouth: "Logan, how are we going to fit in the little house? Are we crazy for wanting to do this? Where are we going to put your tools, the bulk food, and our camping stuff? Are we making the wrong decision?"

"Tammy, don't worry. We can store a lot of stuff under the house. We're gong to fit. You're in freak-out mode. Besides, I'm going to downsize my stuff again."

"Really?" I asked.

"Yes, really. I know I've been slacking off. I haven't tallied up my stuff in a while."

I let out a huge breath, wrinkled my forehead, and said, "Well, that makes me feel a little bit better. I think we should follow Dee's suggestion and tape off the living room floor. Let's measure out the length of the trailer, an eight-by-sixteen-foot area, and visualize our new space. We can set up a pretend tiny house in our apartment. Being able to see all of the stuff might prompt us to donate more stuff to charity."

It was June 2011, and Logan and I had signed a contract with Portland Alternative Dwellings, a small, Portland-based, tiny house company, and committed to building our own tiny house on wheels. We were due to move in by October 2011, and I was panicking. About three years before, Logan and I had done the 100 Thing Challenge after moving from Davis to Sacramento. We inventoried our personal stuff, and enjoyed it, but there's a slight problem with the challenge. It's arbitrary. You can set up your own rules, and at the time I only counted my personal stuff — things like shoes, clothing, books, tech gadgets, and more. Somehow, we never got around to doing the challenge on our household items together.

Now we were moving from what felt like a large 400-square-foot studio to a truly tiny 128-square-foot home, and our downsizing had a new urgency. Since I was so worried about fitting into the little house, we decided to declutter before moving rather than after. As we went through our stuff, we looked at every item and asked ourselves: Do we really need this? Do we use it daily, weekly, or monthly? Can we share tools instead of having our own? Do we really need a personal library or can we donate most of our books to the public library?

It feels good giving stuff away; it's just the in-between process that's difficult. Having stuff out of place and jumbled makes me anxious and grumpy. As we pared down our belongings, I let go of more books and Logan donated a few bike tools to friends. My fear ebbed as we reaffirmed our commitment to living small and thinking big.

This was actually our third experience with the decluttering process. The first time was when Logan and I moved within Davis itself, from a 1,200-square-foot apartment to an 800-square-foot apartment. During that first move, I was having trouble letting go of my stuff, and I figured if I purchased a lot of Storable containers, I could store my stuff under the bed.

Luckily, my friend Allison talked me out of it. She said, "Tammy, what's the point of buying more stuff to store your stuff? Let it go and stay away from Storables. You'll be happier." Allison was right. And my Storables experience was recently echoed by another friend, Matt, as Logan and I prepared to move into our tiny house.

Matt told us that as he prepared to move, he became really overwhelmed as he began pulling stuff out of closets, cupboards, and secret junk drawers. It wasn't until he started packing that he realized how much stuff he owned. Matt looked around his chaotic apartment and said, "I know what the problem is; my stuff is unorganized! I need to go to Storables! Then packing won't be so difficult."

In Storables, Matt wandered up and down the aisles looking at all the different storage options. After about an hour, he felt suffocated by the faint plastic scent and the thousands of storage containers towering above him. He said aloud, "What am I doing here? I'm buying more stuff to store my stuff. This is crazy!"

With that Matt left the store and went home with a new mission. He sold most of his stuff and decluttered his life before he moved. In the end, he made five thousand dollars, moved to a smaller apartment, and used the extra cash to enroll in cooking school. Attending cooking school was a lifelong dream that he finally had the means to make a reality.

Each time I have downsized my life, it has made me happier. I feel like I'm living and not sleepwalking through my daily routine. I frequently remember a powerful talk my friend Dee Williams once gave (through the nonprofit TED organization). Dee introduced us to the idea of a tiny house, and helped us build ours, and in the talk she asked the audience, "Take a moment and think about what thing you want to hold in your arms as you die. What favorite room in your house or space could accommodate that last breath?" If we asked these questions more often, I think we'd stay out of Storables. We'd focus less on stuff and shift our attention toward people and experiences — the things that make us truly happy.

We Are Our Stuff

The morning that I was clearing my bookshelves and panicking about our move to our little house, it was raining hard. As I looked out the window, the water seemed to be coming down in sheets. I'd never seen it rain so hard, which is kind of shocking because it rains all the time in Portland. I momentarily considered bailing on my volunteer commitment that afternoon. The bike ride was long, and

I had a lot of writing to do. Yet I reminded myself that I had brand-new rain pants and that I always felt better after I volunteered. I needed to push through the lazy creep — my name for that feeling that softly nudges me to stay at home with a book and a cup of coffee. Maybe it sounds strange, but cycling in nasty weather inspires me and keeps my ego in check. When the wind and rain hit my face and I'm immersed in nature, it's easy to remember that I'm just one person in a very big world.

I was volunteering at a place called Living Yoga, and by the time I got there, it was raining even harder and the wind was wailing. I entered looking like a wet cat. Beads of rain dropped off my jacket as I took off my layers. I was glad I hadn't succumbed to the lazy creep and grateful to be in the warm office with some of my favorite people in Portland.

After I settled in, Amy, the executive director of Living Yoga, leaned back in her chair and asked me, "Last night a friend and I were talking about how stuff plays such a big role in our lives. What was it like for you donating and selling so many of your possessions?"

I said, "Well, paring down our stuff took a lot of time. It's been a process. Initially we started downsizing to save money. I never imagined that we'd give away most of our stuff and build a tiny house."

"Do you regret giving away any of your stuff?" Amy asked.

"Initially, I thought that I'd regret giving away so much stuff, but it's funny, the more we gave away, the better we felt. The hardest possessions to part with were the cars. The cars were hard to let go of, but we don't miss them. Besides, I love riding my bike, even in the pouring rain."

Amy explained that she'd been decluttering her house and donating a lot of stuff to charity. When she originally moved to Portland, she didn't have much. Now her apartment was filled with stuff, and dealing with it took more time than she liked. Amy said she'd just gone through her fabric and given a lot of it away. She noted, "It was so hard. I love to sew, but I realized that I don't have the time to use all the fabric I collected. If I'm lucky, I can sew one dress a month."

After I left Living Yoga, I kept thinking about why so many people hold on to stuff. I held on to stuff I didn't need or use because I wanted to hold on to that part of my identity, or my perceived identity. I am a writer, a knitter, a doodler, a skier, a hiker, and more. Cool belongings, like fancy skis, seem to represent my personality. But in truth, I hardly ski anymore, so why keep skis? If I accumulate stuff just to prove who I am, or was, it prevents me from doing meaningful things with my life right now, like focusing on health, happiness, and my relationships.

Courtney Carver: Health, Happiness, and Relationships

Courtney's journey toward a simpler life started when she was diagnosed with multiple sclerosis (MS) in 2006. Courtney told me, "I was overwhelmed and didn't know what to think. First, I had to figure out how to take care of myself. So I looked at my diet and then at how I spent money. For whatever reason, the diagnosis pushed me to take the next step and reexamine my life. I didn't want to wait another five years to make a big change. The diagnosis made me realize that nothing is certain. Prior to being diagnosed, it never crossed my mind that I would have to live with a potentially debilitating disease. When I think about my MS diagnosis, I really think it was my body's way of rejecting my lifestyle."

As a result, Courtney changed her lifestyle, and despite dealing with a serious health problem, she's happier than ever. She appreciates the time and energy that come with simplifying your life, which allows her to focus on relationships and doing work she loves. And she hasn't had an MS relapse in three years! Interestingly, like many people with debilitating diseases or disabilities, Courtney has adapted to her MS diagnosis by creating a life that's as or more satisfying than her life before.

A 1978 study by psychologist Philip Brickman has been widely cited in happiness research. In the study, Brickman looked at two groups of people — one group had just been in an accident that left them paralyzed and the other group had recently won the lottery. Right after these events the lottery winners were much happier than the accident victims. As Brickman tracked these groups, something unexpected occurred. He found that the group of lottery winners returned to the same happiness set-point they had had prior to winning the lottery, and the group of accident victims returned to a happiness set-point just slightly lower than they had had before.

This concept is reaffirmed by Paul Martin in his memoir *One Man's Leg*. Martin lost his leg in a car accident and spent over five weeks in the hospital. When it was time to leave, he made himself a commitment: "It was time to go home and start facing the challenge of believing that I, an individual, am not too small to make some sort of positive difference in our world. *My actions can make a difference*, I promised myself. By being myself and setting an example of what it means to see the bright side of every predicament, I can shine a light on the people I meet." Despite the challenges Martin faced, he chose to change his life for the better and find ways to help other people.

It seems that challenges can bring out the best in us. Courtney explained, "After my diagnosis I worried like crazy. In some ways the fear was really worse than the diagnosis because I didn't know how it was going to impact my body. Cutting back on my commitments made me stay more present. Basically, I looked at what I was doing and made time to rest. I'd never done that before. I even took a few naps."

I raised my eyebrows in surprise because I've always been a big fan of naps. Even when I am really busy, I make time to nap. Courtney laughed at my reaction and said, "It was really hard to start taking naps because I was so used to being on the go all the time. Then I started incorporating yoga into my routine, and I slowed down even more."

As she was slowing her life down, Courtney said, the next challenge was paying off debt. Courtney remarked, "I was diagnosed with MS in July 2006, and I started listening to Dave Ramsey's radio show. Hearing the stories of people who were in dire situations and had paid off their debt in a few years was really powerful. I realized that if they could pay off their debt, I could, too." Courtney and her husband had a lot of debt, including car loans, student loans, and two credit cards they used regularly, plus all of the store cards from places like Macy's and the Gap. Courtney said, "I thought I was getting all these great deals and saving so much money, but I couldn't figure out why I was living paycheck to paycheck. I wasn't maxing out my credit cards, but when you do the math and make a twenty- or fifty-dollar payment spread across seven credit cards, that's a lot of money." In the summer of 2010, Courtney paid off the last bit of her consumer debt. Now, the only debt her family has left is their home mortgage, and that might change if they sell the house in the next few years. Courtney observed, "The house is too much in terms of space. In 2005, we bought the house, and it never crossed my mind that we didn't need 2,000 square feet of space. Now we've got rooms that I never enter."

Those rooms weren't empty and unused a few years ago. They were filled with stuff, and even though Courtney has always loved organizing her belongings, she still had trouble finding things because she had so much! Courtney mentioned, "As I simplified, it seemed like there was always more in the back of the closet." Then, she became truly inspired, and in January 2010, she started Project 333.

If you want to pare down your wardrobe, Project 333 is the perfect starting point. Courtney's minimalist fashion project began as a personal experiment to dress with less and to challenge her blog readers, too. The idea is to narrow down your wardrobe to thirty-three pieces of clothing and wear only those items for the next three months. When Courtney started this experiment, she packed up all her excess clothes in boxes and either stored them in the garage or donated them to charity.

When the first three months are done, participants sort through the clothes they have been wearing and build a new thirty-three-piece wardrobe from their current collection. Typically, participants donate a lot of clothes to charity and replace them with new pieces of clothing. As with the 100 Thing Challenge, you can create your own rules as you go. Typically items that are included in Project 333 are clothing, accessories, jewelry, outerwear, and shoes. Things that aren't included? Your wedding ring (or any piece of jewelry that you never take off), underwear, socks, and workout clothing.

Courtney commented, "We still have stuff, and there is a lot more that we can let go of. We've been talking about what we would bring if we moved, and there isn't much I'd want to take with me. The more you let go of, the less you want. I know some people who have decluttered overnight, but that's not me." Downsizing is a process and it can take time. If you give everything away really quickly, the habit might not stick.

I was curious about how Courtney's family felt about her experiments in living with less, especially her daughter and husband. She said, "I've tried to be really respectful of the fact that this is a big change in mindset. I can't make my husband go along on this journey. What's important now is that we have a similar view of the future. We don't want to be married to a mortgage, to debt, or to work until we die."

However, downsizing has naturally influenced everyone's habits. As Courtney paid off her debt and decluttered her life, she shopped less, and the less she shopped, the less she wanted. Now, because Courtney doesn't shop as much, Courtney's daughter naturally shops less, too. And if Courtney's daughter wants anything, it has to be included in the monthly budget. Courtney said, "I'm trying to show her that it's important to plan how you spend money. It's my hope that she doesn't have a credit card in college because that's where it went downhill for me, and I think that's true for a lot of people. You have spending power and start thinking, 'Well, it's only another twenty dollars.' Before you know it, you've got a lot of credit card debt to deal with."

"So have all of these experiments in living with less made you happier?" I asked.

"I'm happier and our family is happier. Before simplifying I had a huge weight on my shoulders. I wanted to retire with style, so I was always worried about our future and money. Now I have a very different picture of what the future looks like. I'm happier doing less and don't need to fill in every second of the day with activities. I was so busy being like everybody else that I forgot what really sang to me. I'm rediscovering the person I always was. I used to think buying things made me happy. I'd wait for big sales at the mall and then bring home my 'kill.' In a few days my high would be over. I don't have the thrill of acquisition anymore, and I don't have the slump afterward. Now I go out and hike instead of going to the mall."

Despite dealing with MS, debt, and a lot of clutter, Courtney has taken one small step every day that's led her to a happier and healthier life and a clear vision of what she wants.

Chris O'Byrne: Remove the Blocks to See

I remember the first time I received an email from Chris O'Byrne a few years ago. I had recently announced on my blog that I was going to publish my first ebook, *Simply Car-Free*, and Chris offered to edit my book for free. I said yes, but that yes was full of hesitation. It boggled my mind that someone would do something like that for free. Chris offered to help me because it was useful editorial training for him. Since then he's edited a number of other projects for me. Typically, we barter. I send him coffee, chocolate, and books, and he edits my ebooks and some blog content.

Since our first project together, Chris has started a company called Red Willow Digital Press, and he's doing exceptionally well. So well, in fact, that he's been able to bring his family into the venture. All of this success came about because he decided to sell most of his stuff and focus on what was important. By shedding his stuff and lowering his expenses, he was able to start a small business and spend more time with his family. Chris literally edited his life.

On a recent trip to Portland, Chris talked with me about downsizing and happiness. The sun was shining in a nearly cloudless sky, so we decided to walk over the Hawthorne Bridge and hang out at Coava Coffee Roasters. It was quiet, the perfect place to chat about happiness, simplicity, and business. I took a sip of my cappuccino and asked Chris my standard question: Has living simply made you happier?

"Nothing *makes* me happy; it's what I am," said Chris, as he took a sip of his coffee. "I find joy and happiness in a lot of things. It's a constant state of being. No matter what's happened in my life, no matter how painful the circumstances, happiness is always there. You know the old saying, 'There is no way to happiness. Happiness is the way.' That's what happiness and simplicity are like for me. Happiness is always there. If it's not, you're allowing something to block you from seeing that it's there. This is the reality of my life — the depth of my happiness."

Chris's comment reminded me of something Yongey Mingyur Rinpoche, a Tibetan Buddhist meditation master and best-selling author, said in his book *The Joy of Living*: "Ultimately, happiness comes down to choosing between the discomfort of becoming aware of your mental afflictions and the discomfort of being ruled by them."

I asked Chris playfully, "Well, that's very Zen. Did you always feel this way?"

Chris chuckled. "About two or three years ago, I had an experience I call an awakening. It was a 'holy shit' kind of moment and it changed everything. After that I could really see what was going on. Everything started to make sense. Along the way, I had been doing little things that helped me remove the blocks from my vision — things like living simply, downsizing my possessions, and working for myself.

"When I look back, I see how my meditation practice set the stage for a shift in my perspective. Awakenings often happen when a significant event occurs; for me it was when my little brother died. When my dad told me, I fell off into nothingness, and it felt like I was there for a long time. I couldn't see anything, only feel. All of those old blocks fell away."

Chris explained that when he "woke up" he felt an "overwhelming sense of bliss, understanding, and peace." He knew what was important and what was silly. He went on to say, "It's the stuff I knew intellectually, but not deep in my core. Happiness is being loving. It's relationships. Nothing more."

I asked, "So after your brother died and you 'woke up,' did you start downsizing?"

"I had been downsizing slowly for a long time because it felt right." Chris smiled. "I have always been impulsive. After my brother died, I started thinking about it more. I knew my stuff was a huge block and I had to remove it."

"You mentioned that happiness is part of who you are, but do you think shedding stuff has made you happier?" I asked.

"Happiness is the underlying stratum, the bedrock of my life. Joy is the gem. It's the scone in the morning. The cappuccino. The oatmeal muffin. Another big joy in my life is accepting other people for who they are and where they're at. It's all these little things. It's not about stuff. There are so many opportunities to practice joy and happiness, and people miss them."

Chris's comments helped me reflect on why I live simply. By letting go of my belongings, I've found a few gems, too — the things you can't buy, like wisdom, joy, and happiness. As my friend Dee said, "Stuff is a huge distraction from your character."

The Comfort of Diamonds

In November 2010, I made the decision to sell my diamond wedding set. As I described in chapter 2, by that time I no longer wore it or needed it, and it only reminded me of the more-materialistic "old Tammy." However, I didn't try to sell the ring immediately. I let it sit in my jewelry box for months, reluctant to act on my decision. Then one day I had a conversation with my friend Michelle. We were sitting in a local bar and she asked, "Tammy, what's the barrier to selling the ring?"

I told Michelle that it boiled down to laziness. It was a whole lot easier to leave the ring in my jewelry box than to put in the legwork to sell it. I didn't want to spend hours calling consignment shops or jewelry stores. Still, I knew in my heart that letting go of the ring was the right thing to do.

Michelle suggested that I hire her boyfriend, Andrew, to help. She remarked, "He's sold a few pieces of jewelry for me, and he has a few connections to local Portland shops. You could give him 10 percent of the sale price."

"That's a great idea, Michelle! Let me talk to Logan and see what he thinks."

Logan also liked the plan. He was happy to support Andrew, since he's a friend, and stated, "It's obvious that you aren't going to sell the ring. You've been sitting on it for the past eight months, and I didn't want to sell it from underneath you. I felt like you might hold it against me."

"I wouldn't hold it against you. The ring isn't important to me anymore. I don't need a ring to show other people that we have a strong marriage. However, I recognize that I'm not going to sell the ring myself. I'm too lazy to do the legwork. I don't know why I didn't think of this before!"

However, I have come to realize that it wasn't laziness that kept me from acting. It was an aversion to loss. Typically, once you've invested in something, you don't want to abandon that investment. Studies have shown that fear of loss is twice as powerful a motivation as the promise of gain. In *How We Decide*, Jonah Lehrer explains, "Loss aversion is now recognized as a powerful mental habit with widespread implications. The desire to avoid anything that smacks of loss often shapes our behavior, leading us to do foolish things." Like leaving one's diamond wedding ring in a jewelry box for years without wearing it.

Despite Andrew's efforts, as of the time of this writing, I still have the ring. We haven't been able to sell it, and other options aren't appealing. We could put it on consignment at a jewelry store, but jewelers usually take a big cut. If we sold it for scrap, it would garner about two hundred dollars; one jeweler said he would probably only take the gold and give us the diamonds back. Logically, I know that I'm not going to recover the entire four-thousand-dollar cost of my wedding set because diamonds don't hold their value over the long run. Diamonds may last forever but their retail value does not. Yet I remain hopeful that someone will consider the set worth more than two hundred dollars. I'm ready to let my wedding ring go, but I'm still averse to a near-total financial loss.

On my blog, I asked readers to share any similar experiences they have had struggling to let go of stuff that didn't serve them anymore. I received many interesting responses, including these two stories:

> We purposefully don't own very much and really had a lot of discussions about whether we "needed" rings. We found a small but beautiful engagement ring at an antiques fair. It was inexpensive, and the stories of the previous owners that accompanied the ring were a huge part of its attraction. It is wonderful to let things go, but sometimes it is also helpful to think about the things you "want" and decide whether there is a way to have what you want without ruining your bank balance, your values, or the environment.

> It makes me sick to think of how much money I spent on certain things that I didn't need or never use. So I just hang on to them to try and squeeze some sort of use or meaning out of them. It's so frustrating! So much of it is tied into my relation to money and a sort of poverty mentality. It doesn't have to do with the item itself; it has to do with my feelings of guilt over spending money when I didn't have much to spend in the first place. I've found that letting go of "things" is so much about self-evaluation, which has been a total surprise to me as I've started the process of downsizing.

Interestingly, researchers from Yale University and the University of New Hampshire published a study in the *Journal of Experimental Social Psychology* about stuff and security. The researchers theorized that people value their belongings because "ownership of goods promotes feelings of security." If that's the case, increasing a person's sense of "security should reduce the value they place on possessions." In the experiments, researchers asked the participants how much they valued specific items, like a blanket or a pen. People who felt loved and accepted by others placed a lower monetary value on their possessions than people who did not.

In their concluding remarks, the researchers said, "The findings seem relevant to understanding why people may hang on to goods that are no longer useful. They also may be relevant to understanding why family members often fight over items from estates that they feel are rightfully theirs and/or to which they are already attached." In other words, people hold on to stuff, not out of laziness, but because it gives them a sense of protection and comfort. I've found this to be true. Buying stuff comforted me and compensated for any feelings of inadequacy.

Micro-actions

As I've mentioned, getting rid of things is a long, ongoing process. Here are some ways to evaluate your things to determine what's not useful anymore and what isn't worth keeping.

- **Evaluate how much time you spend managing your stuff.** How much of your life is dedicated to acquiring and managing your stuff? Quantify this. How long does it take to clean your apartment or house? To clean and maintain your car, your lawn or garden, your appliances, and so on? How much time do you spend managing, cleaning, and maintaining your clothes? Now, which of these areas could be simplified, freeing your life?
- **Evaluate how often you use your stuff.** In each room, as you sort through your stuff, ask yourself: Do I really need

this? Do I use it daily, weekly, or monthly? Could you share tools instead of owning your own set? Could you use the public library instead of buying books and filling your home with a personal library?

- **Sort your stuff into piles.** As you sort through your stuff, create piles. For example, create a donate pile, a trash pile, and an "I don't know" pile. Remember, it's okay to keep or store things. For example, Logan stores his bike tools under our tiny house. You don't have to give everything away. However, it's important for you to figure out what you need and what you don't. Only you can make those decisions.
- **Decide what to do with your stuff.** Now that you've sorted your stuff into piles, decide what you want to do with it. Will you give it to charity or sell it on eBay or Craigslist?
- **Don't fear the trash.** Unfortunately, some things will end up in the trash. For example, I tried to repair clothes and furniture before I donated them. But if my stuff was moth-eaten, it went into the trash. Luckily, most of my old stuff was salvageable.
- **Talk to your partner.** Logan and I have had plenty of fights over stuff, like with our bulk food. We didn't always agree about what was important to keep or get rid of. Yet we were able to talk through our differences, compromise, and still successfully downsize. If you live with a partner, disagreements over what to keep and what to give away are bound to arise. Remember, that's okay. The important thing is to talk through your problems. Keep the lines of communication open.
- **Join Project 333.** If you're thinking of paring down your wardrobe, Project 333 is a great starting point. The idea is to narrow down your wardrobe to thirty-three pieces of clothing and wear only those items for three months. The

project is a lot of fun, and it will make you question how much you really need in your wardrobe.

- **As you let go of stuff, increase self-care.** Brainstorm areas of your life that need a little extra attention. As you simplify your life, think about the things you can do to take care of yourself. Replace stuff with experiences you enjoy. As was the case for Courtney, perhaps that means taking power naps and eating healthy food. Like Chris, perhaps you can meditate more often. Start doing the things you always wished you had time to do.

CHAPTER 6

The Joy of the Small House

If we could just have the kitchen and a bedroom,
that would be all that we'd need.

— JULIA CHILD

The workshop started bright and early on Saturday morning, and Logan and I were getting ready by consuming large quantities of Stumptown coffee. We'd driven up to Portland the day before, and we were both still sleepy and tired from the drive. Now, my heart was pounding, and I had butterflies floating in my stomach. I knew I shouldn't be nervous, but meeting Dee Williams was a big deal. Watching her video in December 2007 on how to construct a tiny house had been a huge turning point for us. After seeing Dee's video, we had written down our long-term goals, and one of those goals was to either buy or build a tiny house. For us, a little house on wheels represented simple living at its best. It was now June 2009, and we were still living in Sacramento. As we drove to the construction workshop in Portland that morning, I was thinking about all kinds of things, like how we would finance our future little abode and whether or not Dee would like us.

When we got out of the car, Dee recognized Logan and me immediately, and she bounded over to greet us with a spring in her step. Dee gave us a big smile and a huge hug. The little crinkles around Dee's mouth made her smile seem even more sincere.

Dee introduced us to Katy Anderson, a talented finish carpenter and co-instructor of the workshop. Then we toured Dee's little house, a teeny-tiny, eighty-four-square-foot home that felt surprisingly roomy. The open loft, ten-foot ceiling, abundant windows, and exquisite skylight gave the house a feeling of spaciousness. I could have gawked over Dee's little house all afternoon, but it was time to start the workshop and learn how to build one of our own.

As the day wore on, the sun beat down on my back and sweat rolled down my forehead, yet the workshop was a blast. All the participants had a great time. We learned a lot about construction, and Dee talked about how it felt to live in such a confined space. More importantly, I learned that I had no desire to build a tiny house myself. One reason we attended the workshop was to figure out if we had the skills and the inclination to be builders. I'm notoriously clumsy, and for me the construction process wasn't intuitive. I'd rather be writing than building. As Logan and I talked about the workshop on our drive back to Sacramento, we decided to hire Dee and Katy to design and build our little house.

During the long trek home, I told Logan, "We just met Dee, but I feel like we've known her for a long time. She has such a big heart and is so generous. She seems to fundamentally understand that strong relationships are the source of happiness."

Soon after the workshop, I interviewed Dee for my blog, and we talked about the relationship between living simply and happiness. She said, "I think my smaller life has offered me a clearer picture of the difference between what I want and what I need. That discourse doesn't always make me calm or happy; it challenges me. That said, living small does bring a certain satisfaction and awareness to life — a certain 'ah-haaa' when you recognize that you don't really need a bigger house or more stuff to be in love with your life. I have wonderful neighbors, a nice garden, the food co-op is only a few blocks away, there are bats that swing by at dusk, herons and whales just down the hill in Puget Sound, rain on the roof, wind in the eaves, sunflowers coming up in the garden — all sorts of things that make my life so incredibly gifted. All that makes me crazy happy."

Dee's comments reminded me of my paternal grandparents, who believed a home didn't have to be extravagant or large so long as you felt comfortable and secure.

Happiness in 600 Square Feet

How much space do you need to be happy? In the 1950s, the average size of the American home was 983 square feet. By 1970, it had grown to 1,400 square feet, and by 2004, it had expanded to more than 2,300 square feet. There's nothing wrong with space in and of itself, but space costs money. Over the same time period, as average home sizes more than doubled, median home prices more than tripled (even adjusted for inflation). Part of the American story is that bigger is better, and with cheap credit and tax breaks for home buyers, it's tempting to stretch one's finances to build or buy a larger house.

My dad's parents chose a different path. Once they factored in the interest on a mortgage, property taxes, insurance, utilities, and upkeep, they realized that the best choice for their own well-being would be to pay cash. To do that, they'd have to build their own "little house." They didn't want to find themselves working longer and longer hours just to pay for more space and the stuff to fill it.

My grandparents Mabel and Otto first met in a small coffee shop off College Avenue in Berkeley, California. Mabel was a café waitress, and in my imagination I see her pouring Otto a steaming cup of coffee and taking his order. He looks up, immediately smitten. My grandma was beautiful, and she always had a wide smile and a twinkle in her big blue eyes.

When I asked my dad about my grandparents' first meeting, he said, "I don't know all the specifics, but I'm sure Grandpa was feeding his face, and they got acquainted." Dad continued, "Dating was more formal at that time. Your great-aunt Mamie was their supervisor. At least until they got married in January of 1932." Mabel and Otto married during the Great Depression. They didn't have a whole lot of money, so Grandpa quit college and became a dockworker in Oakland.

My grandparents both grew up in farming communities and within very large families, so living simply was integral to their life philosophy. In the 1950s, when my dad was a little boy, my grandparents built a 600-square-foot cottage. They put the twenty-by-thirty-foot structure on a small plot of land in Pleasant Hill, which they bought for six hundred dollars. They paid cash for everything.

Dad remarked, "Reusing and recycling was a necessity. In essence, they were recycling before it became 'cool.'" Grandpa Otto got most of the materials for their little house by scrounging the Oakland docks. The paneling came from old grain doors, and the two-by-fours were reclaimed from old army lockers. He even found some sheets.

It took four years to build the small cottage, and when they moved in, the roof wasn't even on! Finishing the house took a lot of time because my grandmother was in and out of the hospital a lot. They had to pay in cash for the hospital visits, and this depleted the house fund.

My dad recalled sleeping in the house as a twelve-year-old kid and looking up at the stars. Dad didn't mind living in an unfinished house. He described Pleasant Hill as "open and private. It felt like all the homes were on ten acres." Dad used to ride his bike from Pleasant Hill to Walnut Creek, and it was all farmland. He said, "At that time Walnut Creek was just a one-street city. I used to play touch football with friends in the walnut orchards. Now that isn't possible for kids because every square inch of space has been used. During this time the guys with the GI Bill were starting to migrate to the suburbs, and the town began to expand."

Over the years my dad and grandparents noticed dramatic changes in their community. Each year more farmland was devoured to build strip malls and neighborhoods with larger homes. As real estate prices rose, many of their neighbors sold their homes and lots. Soon my grandparents had the only small house on the block, surrounded by a sea of homes four times the size of their dwelling. Yet my grandparents loved their little home and were content with what they had. Even though the house was small, it didn't feel cramped. As my dad said, "Everyone was happy and content. The size of the house didn't matter."

My grandparents taught me that living a simple life isn't about self-deprivation. Instead, it's about giving yourself the time, freedom, and money to pursue your dreams. In many ways, I've modeled my life after that of my grandparents. I learned from them that simplicity isn't about austerity. It's a revolution in personal growth.

Andrew Odom: A Tiny r(E)volution

Andrew Odom is the man behind a blog called Tiny r(E)volution. A thirty-three-year-old social media manager, he loves tiny homes, farming, and the simple life. Andrew remarked, "We don't label ourselves as minimalists, homesteaders, or tinyhousers. We're just a family, and it just so happens our family fits nicely into those boxes." He and his wife, Crystal, have a brand-new baby named Tilly Madison, and we got a chance to talk about all things tiny in mid-2011.

Andrew explained, "Crystal and I grew up on the poor side of things. I had five siblings, and she had three. I grew up in Virginia, and she grew up in North Carolina. Our parents worked all the time to provide the few things we had. I grew up in a 1,070-square-foot home with three bedrooms. My room was so small it only accommodated a bunk bed. My dad was a firefighter, and he made about thirty-five thousand dollars a year. Crystal's parents were tobacco farmers. During the off-season they took whatever job was available. We both tried to escape the South and headed as far away as we could. I went to Boston, and Crystal went to Miami. We were doing the normal college thing and both figured we'd get married, buy a house with a white picket fence, and have kids. We hadn't met but we were on the same path."

Eventually, Andrew and Crystal did meet and become friends. He said, "We both got bit by the travel bug and spent the next six years traveling to twenty-seven countries and witnessing everything. We became missionaries with one of the largest Christian churches in the world."

After traveling with the church, Andrew got involved with an Internet-based business. "I answered a job-board posting to work with a start-up, and it was a lot of fun. That start-up turned out to be Skype. That was my first taste of freedom and money. And that's what I wanted — money and freedom."

Unfortunately, Andrew lost his job. One day, to get his mind off his worries, he attended a college football game. He said, "There was this guy who introduced me to the world of credit. I didn't have a job and this guy was offering me five thousand dollars. Once I got that card, I took people out to dinner, went shopping, and bought gas. It turned into less about getting by and more about getting myself into the hole."

Eventually Andrew moved to Brooklyn for work. "That's where I met this old black guy who was growing tomatoes in buckets. He grew up in Alabama, and I could see the tomatoes were more than just tomatoes — they were something much more. The tomatoes represented home. It didn't matter if he grew anything. It was a connection for him." Andrew's interests started to shift; he became fascinated with the idea of growing his own food and building a home of his own.

Around the same time, Andrew's job in Brooklyn started winding down, and he "reconnected with Crystal through the magic of Facebook." She was working in Florida as a manager at a hotel, and they hit it off quickly. But to Crystal, Andrew seemed very stressed out. He noted, "I realized through my conversations with Crystal that I wanted to find freedom again. I had been running ever since I left high school. I wanted to be free, but I was becoming more and more enslaved to the stuff and debt around me."

They decided to move back to the South and get married. Temporarily, they moved into Andrew's parents' house, a recently built 3,600-square-foot home. Andrew said, "Building a big house is something they always dreamed about, but it came true at the expense of other dreams. They are handcuffed to their house payments. So I asked myself, *Do you really want to be landlocked to house payments?*"

At this point, Andrew said, his life "really started" and he found his calling. It all started with a tiny garden in his parents' yard. His dad had never been able to grow watermelons in this particular plot, but Andrew told his dad, " 'I'm going to get stuff to grow.' I didn't know anything about gardening, and I used social media to gather all the information I could. By the end of the summer, I had grown both watermelons and cantaloupes. I told my dad, 'This is what I'm supposed to do.' I knew I had to pay off my debt first, though."

Andrew and Crystal broke down their budget and started

paring back; when I talked with Andrew, his family was seven months away from being debt-free. Andrew emphasized, "It's been a huge undertaking, and we sacrificed a lot, but the funny thing is we don't miss any of it. It's just the nostalgia of the stuff that I miss."

Meanwhile, as they worked toward paying off their debt, Andrew continued learning about gardening and homesteading. Soon they started thinking about buying a house. He said, "We talked to a real estate agent and found a cute little house for $98,000. Then we started talking about financing. The bank told us they were willing to offer us a $160,000 loan, and we got really scared. So we said thank you, but no thank you."

Soon after they said no to the big loan, Crystal sent Andrew an email about tiny house pioneer Jay Shafer and his company, Tumbleweed Tiny Homes. Andrew said, "We checked out the Tumbleweed site and watched a few videos. It was a eureka moment for us! We realized we could own a house. In my parents' house, we were confined to a bedroom and shared everything else. We were already living small, but the tiny house concept was much cooler."

Andrew and Crystal have a deep faith, and he said, "We prayed about the transition to come. We also believe in the power of word. We started saying things like, 'When we build the tiny house....' Or 'When we move into the tiny house....' There were a lot of positive messages. One night we sat down and created a scrapbook, where we put inspiring quotes and sketches of the little house. Then we sat down and explained the idea to my parents."

At first Andrew's parents thought the idea was crazy. They asked: "What if you want to have kids? What if you want to entertain? What about guests?" Andrew looked at his parents and replied, "What if we don't want to be in debt?" Andrew said the room fell completely silent.

Andrew explained to his parents that a tiny house would give them shelter, the ability to travel, and more importantly the ability *not* to work. Andrew said, "I want to be free to not work. I want to work because it's my choice to work, and that's where Tiny r(E)volution began." The blog title emphasizes his frame of mind — that his journey isn't a revolution but an evolution. Andrew aptly noted, "You evolve as you grow."

Since I don't have kids, I always wonder how parents with children approach downsizing and the challenges of family life in a tiny house.

Andrew explained, "The difficulty comes in terms of preparation and the transition to a life with less stuff. For example, we don't have a nursery. Our nursery is a Pack 'N Play. It has everything you need — a changing area, sleeping area, and play area. It's all one unit, and you can easily pack it up and take it on a trip. Someone recently asked me, 'Now that you have a baby, don't you think you're missing out?' And I said, 'Not at all! I walk out onto our front porch every morning and I can breathe, and my baby can go outside and breathe. You can see the dew on the ground in the early morning and listen to the world. There is nothing else blocking me, and that's what I want to give my child. We've just gotten to the place where we can give our child what she needs.' "

Andrew continued, "It's truly Crystal who meditates on these things, and she supports me so I can come up with the 'how-to.' She's the dreamer and I'm the doer. We're going to build a small house on wheels ourselves. Right now we're living in a small bungalow next door to my brother-in-law. It's only 210 square feet. One day I said, 'Wouldn't it be great if we turned the woodshed into an apartment?' And we did it! The bungalow has a water hookup, a shower, a kitchenette, my work space, a little nursery, and the front porch."

Andrew and Crystal love the little bungalow and are in the process of building a tiny house on wheels. I laughed when Andrew said, "We don't know what we're doing, but I have some construction experience. My brother-in-law designs and builds living quarters on small ships. We don't know what the tiny house will look like, but that's part of the adventure. It will be custom built based on our family's needs."

I asked Andrew if he had any take-away tips for parents.

"The best advice I've ever gotten is this — don't let the world speak for you. Don't let the world tell you that you have to have a nursery or you have to outfit your child in Baby Gap. Make your own decisions based on your own life. We have a five-day-old daughter who takes up very little space in this world. My theory is this: we need homes that fit a family, rather than making your family fit in a home."

Andrew also noted, "Relationships are strengthened in smaller dwellings. If Crystal and I are mad at each other, the space makes us confront the problem. We have to say, 'Hey, you hurt my feelings.' Or to be able to humble ourselves and apologize."

Finally, he emphasized the importance of community. He wants to raise kids in a style that "is interactive with other people." Interacting with other people enables kids, Andrew said, "to be more respectful in terms of proximity and space. You don't have to teach them through spanking or verbal discipline because they have an understanding of what it means to live with other people. We think we can autocorrect everything by spanking children and that isn't realistic. If we want to raise our children in a community, we have to expose them to it."

As my conversation with Andrew made clear, what makes a home is the attitude of the people in it, not the size of the space.

What's a Home?

I closed the front door and smiled. I was in Dee's little house, and it was time for bed. I climbed the wooden loft ladder, and when I got to the top, I plopped down on the bed and looked out the window. I pulled back the quilt and shimmied in between the sheets. It wasn't cold but the light rain made the air moist and cool, and I wanted to snuggle under the covers.

It was August 2011, and Logan and I were in the middle of building our tiny house. I decided to spend the weekend with Dee in Olympia and Logan was still at our apartment in Portland. He planned on arriving in Olympia early the next day with the house's wool insulation.

That afternoon, Dee and I had driven up to Gig Harbor together and helped build the floor of the little house. As I thought about the day, I let out a sigh of relief. It felt good to be warm, safe, and cozy. I felt extra lucky because Dee let me sleep in her little house. I watched the light rain hit the skylight and looked out over her neighbor's backyard. The light cast a strange glow onto the grass, like the orange glow from jack-o'-lanterns.

The more time I spent in little homes like Dee's, the more excited I got about moving into our own. Yet I couldn't help but wonder, what would the reality be like? We wanted our little house to fit us like a glove, to be a space for living that would stretch us in the ways we wanted, in the best ways.

Shouldn't a home facilitate these kinds of desires? Shouldn't it be a gateway to the best things in life, like spending time with friends and family? Lying in Dee's loft, I could feel that a home doesn't have to be large to provide a sense of security, warmth, and comfort. A tiny dwelling encourages quiet, listening, and contemplation. A tiny dwelling, we hoped, would be our ticket to rest, relaxation, and financial freedom.

As I watched the rain, a memory resurfaced. I was about seven years old, and Grandma Mabel's television reception started to go out. I walked over to the television and started banging the top with my tiny fist. This was standard operating procedure. We tried adjusting the rabbit ears, but most of the time that didn't work. Inevitably, Grandma or I would go over and start pounding on the TV. After about thirty seconds, the TV's static would be replaced by the latest soap opera.

Grandma Mabel loved watching soap operas; one of her favorite programs was *As the World Turns*. When I was a little girl, we'd sit together on her green love seat and watch the dramas unfold. I remember one episode in particular — the actress was talking about tatami mats and how she wanted to include them in the design of her new mansion. I was intrigued and asked my grandma what they were. She said the mats were made for traditional Japanese-style rooms and were usually made out of straw.

Lying in Dee's loft, I imagined my grandmother giggling over the news that we were planning on living in a tiny house. I'm sure she'd have also been tickled that it would be no bigger than the tatami-bedecked maid's quarters on *As the World Turns*. But I'm sure she'd understand why we chose to live in such a small dwelling.

Life in a Tiny Home

When I told my landlord that Logan and I were moving out, he asked, "Could you tell me why you chose to build a small house on wheels instead of repurposing an existing travel trailer?"

This is a good question, one that others have asked us. In fact, we looked at travel trailers, like Air Streams and a variety of RVs, but they weren't right for several reasons. First, they didn't appeal to me aesthetically. The metal Air Stream trailers felt cold and unwelcoming, and I didn't like the amount of plastic used in traditional RVs. In addition, they generally aren't built for year-round use, whereas our little house is constructed like a normal house. It's built to the International Building Code (IBC), which was developed by the International Code Council and is used throughout the United States. In contrast to an RV, our little house is built for a wide range of climates; it's a cozy cabin on wheels designed exactly to our specifications. The interior is lined with unfinished pine and fir cabinetry, providing lots of storage space. We don't have a lot of stuff — not anymore — but we still need places for our clothes, books, kitchen stuff, camping gear, and bulk food. In short, our home is safe, innovative, affordable, movable, and supercute.

We decided to build our home with wheels so that we could move our house easily if we wanted to. We don't anticipate moving a lot. However, if we decide to move to a different area of Portland or back to California someday, we can easily take our home with us. We don't have to worry about selling it. Instead, we can tow it to our new city.

From an environmental perspective, living in a tiny house means having a relatively low carbon footprint, but that is more a side benefit than our main reason for choosing it. Still, we care about the environment, so we did our best to choose recycled materials and renewable resources in the building process. For example, the walls are insulated with wool insulation from Oregon Shepherd, a company located about forty miles northwest of Portland. Wool insulation is awesome because it's local, nontoxic, and a wonderful alternative to plastic/fiberglass.

We decided to move into this home because it's affordable and it's a perfect urban infill option. For instance, the total cost to build our little house was thirty-three thousand dollars, which included labor and materials. That may seem like a lot of money to spend on such a tiny dwelling, but in the grand scheme of things it's not bad. For us, it's equivalent to about three years' worth of rent. Over time, the low cost of the tiny house will enable us to save and give more to charity.

Just how big is it? About the size of a large car parking space. It's 8 feet wide, 16 feet long, and 13.5 feet tall, and it's roughly 128 square feet. It sounds supersmall, but the height and windows make the house seem much larger on the inside. The house also has a cute little porch that extends outward about a foot from the front door. With a small window in the front door and two windows on either side, the house almost looks like it's smiling at me when I walk up to the front door.

When you walk through the front door, the kitchen is on the left and the bathroom is on the right. Straight ahead against the back wall is our window nook. Typically, the first thing guests notice is the woodsy smell. The interior paneling was constructed with unfinished, knotty pine. So it smells wonderful!

The window nook is awesome because it serves many purposes. It's a great reading area and underneath is storage space. Plus it doubles as a single bed. By sliding the sitting platform out, you have a sleeping space for company! In addition, on the side of the house next to the window nook, French doors make the space feel even more open.

We have a lot of storage in our tiny kitchen. For example, we have a shelf above our kitchen counter that holds glasses, dishes, and other goodies. Right below that shelf we installed mason jars to hold spices, coffee, and tea. It's a great way to keep bottles and jars off the counter. In addition, we have a magnetic block that holds knives, scissors, and other kitchen tools. These solutions are visually appealing and save space. Also, we have a cute little freestanding oven with a two-burner stove top (an Origo 6000) that's used predominately on boats. It uses alcohol as fuel, so it's safe to burn indoors with minimal ventilation. One of my favorite parts of the kitchen is the bamboo countertop and the sink. The sink is made out of recycled copper and is a lovely centerpiece.

The loft is above our kitchen. It's cozy, warm, and a perfect space for sleeping in such tiny quarters. By using vertical space, the loft is a great solution to create more room in our tiny house. Finally, our tiny bathroom uses a composting toilet and has a shower. However, Logan typically showers at the office, and I shower at the gym. This is easier for us, and we don't have to worry about cleaning the shower as often; it's something I loathe.

Since the house doesn't take up much space, it's great for cities, and it would be a fantastic way to increase urban density, especially as an alternative to apartments. Think about all the huge backyards and vacant city lots in America that could be turned into communities specifically for little homes. Designers created suburbia, so why can't space be created for little homes that are affordable and beautiful?

Right now, our little house is nestled in a backyard in north Portland. We pay our friends rent in exchange for a small portion of their yard and for access to water, garbage, and electricity services. We're within a mile of a grocery story and very close to public transit, bike lanes, and downtown Portland. Logan has a six-mile bike commute to his office and loves every minute of it. We're finding that our tiny house really does fit our unique needs. It enables us to create the kind of home and lifestyle we want and to give back to our community.

Simplifying and downsizing your life doesn't necessarily mean living in a tiny house. It's the philosophy of prioritizing happiness and actively shaping your life and circumstances so that you can focus on what truly matters.

Micro-actions

Whether your home or apartment is small by choice or necessity, it doesn't have to feel cramped. Little dwellings can feel open and spacious; it's just a matter of designing them well. Logan and I have taken many tiny actions to make our home feel comfortable and welcoming. As Antoine de Saint-Exupéry said, "You know you have reached perfection of design, not when you have nothing more to add, but when you have nothing more to take away."

- **Create a detailed list of all the activities you do in your home.** If your home feels uncomfortably small, rethink your living space, and perhaps redesign how you use it. What rooms do you spend the most time in, and for what? For a week, keep track of where you go and what you do in your house. Be as specific as possible. If there's no good "place" for a certain activity (like a home office), consider how to utilize spaces differently to do double duty and make room. On the other hand, if you find there are rooms or spaces you rarely use, try cleaning them out and closing them off. Doing this in our apartment made me realize I could live in a smaller space; maybe you can, too.
- **When you come home, put your stuff away immediately.** After living in our tiny house for a few months, I noticed that if I didn't put away my stuff immediately, the house soon looked like a bomb went off. Even a small space is relaxing if it's neat and clean, while clutter piles can ruin my peace of mind and make any space unlivable. Avoid the temptation to leave your stuff on the counter.
- **Make sure each of your belongings has a designated home.** I stay neat by having a designated spot for everything: my computer, power cords, tech devices, clothing, and books. Putting stuff away saves me time because I don't spend fifteen minutes searching for my keys or iPhone every morning. More than that, my things are not in the way, or in Logan's way, when we want to do something else in the space. The trick is forming a ritual of picking stuff up and putting it away.

- **Have fewer, more multipurpose items.** Every kitchen needs cookware and dining ware, but how much of it do you use regularly? Declutter by winnowing a dozen coffee mugs to three, eight plates to four, and so on. If your apartment doesn't fit more than four people, do you need silverware for twenty? For appliances and cookware, use multipurpose items to keep your kitchen clutter-free. Two or three well-designed pots and pans will usually serve most cooking needs. For instance, Logan and I got rid of our coffee maker and instead make coffee in insulated Kleen Kanteens, which we can also drink from and then wash to use later as water bottles.
- **Take advantage of vertical space.** In our tiny kitchen, we maximize storage space and keep our counters clear by putting most things on the wall. As I've described, we use shelves and a magnetic block; these solutions are visually appealing and save space. In addition, our sleeping loft is above our kitchen, which maximizes the living area.
- **Get creative and use space-saving containers.** Okay, Storables isn't all bad. Creative organizational solutions can help you rethink and reuse your space more efficiently and effectively. For instance, for our silverware, we used to use a typical flat plastic drawer organizer. Now we use a wooden holder that sits upright in one of our cabinets. This both keeps the silverware cleaner and opens up a drawer to store towels and napkins.

CHAPTER 7

Reclaiming Work

If you can imagine it, you can achieve it;
if you can dream it, you can become it.

— William Arthur Ward

Living in our tiny house has given me the freedom to reclaim my work life. At one time, I dreaded my job, but I felt I couldn't quit because I needed the money. My cost of living was too high, and it took away my freedom and flexibility to engage in more meaningful, if less lucrative, pursuits. Now, by keeping my expenses low, I can pursue not only a more satisfying job, and even career, but also what I'd consider my "calling," those things that fill me with a sense of true purpose. This is the greatest gift of simplifying one's life.

Chris O'Byrne: Editing Work and Life

I introduced Chris O'Byrne in chapter 5, and his story is a perfect example of how to create a more meaningful work life. As Chris downsized and simplified, he began to rethink his employment.

Rather than dreading going to the office every day, he wanted to be excited about what he did to earn money.

So Chris decided to go into business for himself. Since December 2009, he's built a successful editing and digital publishing business, Red Willow Digital Press, that allows him to work from anywhere. He told me over coffee, "Editing is a skill that I've kept with me over the years, and it's something I really enjoy. I've chosen work that gives me freedom. I still work really hard, but I do it because I enjoy it. Also, I don't hesitate to put it down to spend time with my kids and grandkids. I've chosen work that enables me to do that. It gives me temporal freedom."

For years, Chris worked as a chemical engineer, and then he worked as a teacher. Downsizing his life allowed him to change his career and how his personal life was structured, too. As Chris said, "I can't live my happiness and do something that I hate. Going back to working a nine-to-five job and having to obey someone else's rules would be painful for me. So I don't do it. Living my happiness means working for myself and embracing my love of travel. For years I struggled with that because everyone told me that I *should* settle down, and that was painful. Now, I live with very few possessions and move a lot. I'm not running from anything. I'm moving toward new people and new opportunities. It's my happiness to choose to live close to my family as often as possible and to travel, too."

Today, Chris lives in a rental apartment and works from home. In essence, he's traveling as he works, bringing his office with him as he goes to new places. He's newly remarried, and his kids from his first marriage are now fully grown with their own families. Since they live in different areas of the country, Chris visits his kids frequently. For example, he's spent the past few months living in Arizona, and he's heading back to Minnesota to visit family for a few months. In the fall, he and his wife, Mara, will be moving to Moscow, Idaho.

When his kids were little, it was hard for Chris to "cultivate a work-life balance." He was going to school, working, and spending hours every night doing homework. He felt like he never had enough time with his kids. Chris explained, "When I think about their younger years, I feel sad for me and for them. We didn't get to spend enough time together because I worked a lot. Now I've chosen to live really close to them. They are only a few houses down, and we have a deeper relationship."

In fact, now that his children are adults, Chris has included them in his editing business, working as full-time editors and designers and doing ebook conversions, too. They all work hard and are able to share the workload; that way they don't have to work really long hours. This is another powerful way Chris is living his happiness.

I asked, "What's it like working with your kids?"

Chris sipped his coffee and said, "It's been a process of looking at their strengths and what they do well. I want them to enjoy life. They see how simply I live, and they want that, too. I don't want them to go back to work. I'm not saying this is how you should live, but you should have the opportunity to decide. Our goal is to live simply and not work more than four hours a day. That way my kids have time to spend with their children and to pursue other interests. In some ways the business is like an intentional community, but it's all family. For example, we do everything by consensus decision making. Before I make any decision about the business, I consult with them."

Chris's story illustrates the brilliance of living simply — it allows you to create your own lifestyle, one with the freedom, money, and time to do what you love for a living. Reclaiming work is about doing smart work, having the freedom to set your own schedule, learning to think of work as play, and looking for opportunities in transitions.

Tina's Story: Opportunities in Transition

My sister-in-law Tina, her husband, Tyler, and their two young children, Isaac and Ella, live in an 1,100-square-foot house in Chico, California. Since Tina's house is about eight times the size of our house, she wasn't sure if her story was right for this book, but it is. Ultimately, the size of our dwelling isn't what matters. What matters is rethinking our choices to increase our happiness and sense of community, and in this way, Tina is a great example of an increasingly common modern dilemma.

Tina explained, "It's funny. Everyone asks me, 'How can you live in such a tiny house?' I laugh because I always think about your tiny house. We used to have a vision of a two-story dream house. We wanted a den and a library and all of these other little rooms. I'm a clean freak, and with two kids it would be difficult keeping up with that space. I love having a small house. It's easy to clean. We've thought about moving somewhere outside the city to have more land space. If we built a new house, it would be the same size. The space is perfect for us."

Tina earned a master's degree in school psychology from California State University, Chico. While she was still in college, she worked for three years as a school psychologist at every grade level. When she left school, she became a school counselor for a year and a half and then worked as a school psychologist for six months, working with elementary and junior high students. She loved her career, but after the birth of her first child, she and Tyler looked at the numbers and started to think about whether she should stay at home with the kids. Every type of care situation seemed like it would eat up most of her paycheck.

Tina explained, "Typically, you pay babysitters by the hour, and there were a lot of people who wouldn't commit to full days. Then we started looking into day care and the price was astronomical. I make about a hundred dollars an hour, but after taxes and insurance I realized the cost of working wasn't worth it. I would be paying someone to watch my child, and I would give up that time. That is a huge loss. I felt like it would be a hobby job. I stepped back and asked myself, 'How hard would it be for me to stay at home?' I had a great job with the best benefits in the world, and it was hard to give that up."

They considered whether it made more sense for Tyler to become a stay-at-home parent instead, but Tyler had business opportunities through his job that they wanted to take advantage of, and besides, Tina admitted, "I always imagined staying at home with our kids. I also wondered if this would be an opportunity to really explore other possibilities related to my field. At the time I quit, the schools were getting rather depressing."

At the same time, Tina and Tyler went through their budget and looked at their spending patterns. She said, "We were paying for a gym membership we never used, the TV, plus the satellite, the bug person to come and spray, and a lot of extra expenses like tech stuff. Cutting these costs freed up the money I would be working to pay for. So we gave up those services every month and also factored my drive time. I had to drive forty-five minutes to get to my work site, so we had to consider gas and insurance. We broke everything down by category and looked at what we were using."

Today, Tina saves even more money by making her own cleaning supplies, shopping at the farmer's market, and ordering a few supplies online.

Tina remarked, "I never imagined I'd be a stay-at-home mom. In the beginning it was hard. I had to deal with my own guilt. I place a lot of value on working and earning my keep. I've been working since I was very young. When I was in high school, I had two jobs because I was saving for college, and during college I had a full course load and a full-time job. Staying at home was a huge transition. I went through a time period where I was trying to make my house superawesome, yet dealing with the depression of not knowing if I was doing a good job as a mom. I wasn't happy right away, and I second-guessed every single choice I made. With anything, you really have to evaluate why you're unhappy. One thing I realized was that making the decision to stay at home helped me better organize our lives. When I was working, I felt stressed out and overwhelmed by all the tasks, like cleaning."

As Tina dealt with depression and the stress of being a new mom, she started blogging as a way to reflect on her struggles. Tina said, "I ended up writing humorous blog posts about how hard it is to be a parent and what it's like working with kids. Then I ended up selling one of the stories to *Chicken Soup for the Soul* and started writing for e-how.com. I loved my job as a school psychologist, but now I write because it makes me happy."

Tina made the decision to leave the traditional workforce five years ago. She noted, "Now my friends are starting to make these choices, too, and have asked how we did it. Some of my friends are making less money or they have lost a job, so they are forced to reexamine their choices."

During our conversation, Tina emphasized the importance of examining choices and redefining what you really want out of life. She noted, "You just have to reframe the 'why' and list the reasons why something might be challenging. Everyone has valid and realistic reasons, but sometimes it's important to step back and ask the why question."

Redefining Success: Leaving Cubicle Nation

After graduating from California State University (CSU) with a bachelor of arts in economics and a master's degree in public administration, I got a "real job" at Franklin Templeton Investments as a "futures associate" in a management-training program. It was a unique position because every four months I would be rotated to a new department in the company. I got experience as a supervisor and project manager. At first I was excited about driving to work and the status of my new position. Friends and family members were impressed by my new job. Unfortunately, the honeymoon period didn't last very long. After about two months in the job, I started having back problems because I was sitting too much (both at work and during my commute), and I started to medicate myself, and avoid my true feelings, through shopping and drinking too much wine in the evenings.

As the year went on, I became more depressed. I would call Logan on coffee and lunch breaks in tears. At the time I couldn't articulate why I was so unhappy. On the surface, I was living "the American dream," but underneath I felt like I was stuck in quicksand. The quicker I moved, the faster I got sucked into a hole of depression. Because of our debt, I felt like I didn't have any options. But Logan encouraged me, saying, "There are always options. The options might not be sexy or easy, but they are present."

At Logan's suggestion, I started taking baby steps to change my life. While I was still working for Franklin Templeton, I started getting more exercise, journaling, and eating healthier foods, slowly replacing my bad habits with healthy ones.

As these small steps became my routine, my depression abated, and I started to feel curious, happy, and excited again. My first big decision was to leave the investment management industry and return to graduate school. In the fall of 2005, I started a second master's degree, this one in education, at California State University, Sacramento. Rather than spending my life working with money and numbers, I wanted to work with people. I brainstormed new careers that were closer to my dreams, like victim advocacy, teaching, and writing. I didn't want a "job"; I wanted to find my calling. This change coincided with our downsizing.

During my time at CSU, I enrolled in a peer-counseling training program and started volunteering at a local rape crisis center. Instead of pushing paper around and pretending to do "work," I was constantly learning new things in my classes and helping people in my spare time. I felt energized and useful, instead of drained and depressed, and it all started by redefining my version of success.

After graduation, I started working in the movement to end violence against women. For six years, as a volunteer and staff member, I did everything from counseling to research to public-policy advocacy. I loved the work, but eventually I felt burned out. I knew it was time to make another career change. I wanted to set up a life in which I had more freedom — a life that didn't require clocking in every day or sitting under fluorescent lights. By this time, it was 2010 and we were living in Sacramento. Logan and I had paid off our debt and had built a savings account. I could take a big risk and start my own business as a writer.

The Blog

In 2004, as I became depressed about my financial industry job, I started journaling as a way to rethink my life. I found I enjoyed writing. Over time, it helped me think about everything Logan and I were going through: the journey of downsizing and redesigning our lives. By 2007, after spending a few years working as a victim advocate, I decided I wanted to write on a more regular basis, both to improve my writing and to connect with like-minded people. Blogging seemed the perfect medium, but at the time I had no idea how to "blog." I only used the Internet for research.

In December 2007, I took another baby step when I created RowdyKittens.com. I wanted a blog name that was memorable, represented my personality, and would make my readers smile. There is so much bad news in the world, and I wanted a fun blog name to combat all the negativity. One day in a conference room, I was talking with a few coworkers about how I didn't know what to name my new blog. I asked for suggestions, and one person shouted, "Rowdy," another said, "Kittens," and thus, the name RowdyKittens was born.

In the beginning I only had a few readers. I remember getting excited when my readership doubled — going from two readers to four. Surprisingly, that didn't include my parents. When I told my mom about my blog, she looked at me and asked, "What's a blog?"

As I put more time into my writing, the site slowly grew, little by little. Eventually, my mom started reading my writing, too! By 2008, I was thinking about starting my own writing business. Creating an online business would give me more freedom and flexibility. I imagined selling ebooks and creating a membership site where readers received weekly articles for a small fee; I also hoped to make money as a freelance writer for other online sites and magazines. I'd be able to structure my day in ways that fostered my creativity, rather than being locked into a nine-to-five schedule. I wasn't sure if I could make it work, but I wanted to give it a shot. The timing was perfect. Logan and I had been talking about moving to the Pacific Northwest for years, and in July 2010 he was set to finish up his PhD. With so many good things on the horizon, we decided to take a big risk and move to Portland in early 2010.

We chose Portland because the city appealed to us, especially its bike infrastructure, good public transportation, plethora of small businesses, and large parks. It felt like a home away from home. Before our move, I quit my job at the California Coalition Against Sexual Assault and focused on my blog and other writing projects. During the first year on my own I made just over twenty thousand dollars. We were also planning our move into our tiny house, which would downsize our expenses even further. I wasn't sure I'd be successful as a writer, but we were creating a situation in which I could continue trying.

In the summer of 2010, I woke up to a surprise. We had been in Portland for five months and were living in a small, studio apartment. As usual, I stumbled out of bed, made a little pot of coffee, and logged into my email account. One email stood out: an interview request from Stephanie Rosenbloom, a *New York Times* reporter. Stephanie said that she was writing an article about happiness and downsizing and wondered if she could interview me over the phone.

A little voice in the back of my head said, "Why would she want to talk to me? I'm not that interesting. What if she includes me in the story and people think I'm crazy?" But I pushed those fears aside and said yes.

During the interview, Stephanie and I chatted about all kinds of topics relating to simplicity. I didn't think the story would be a big deal; I figured it would be buried in the back of the paper. Afterward, Stephanie emailed that she wanted to send a photographer to our apartment, and I had a feeling the article might be bigger than I expected.

The story ended up running on the front page of the *New York Times*' Sunday business section, and it remained the top emailed story for several weeks! As a result of the article, Logan and I received a lot of media inquiries about our story, and we appeared on the *Today* show, CNN, MSNBC, and more. Within a few days, I'd received over a dozen requests from literary agents asking if I'd like to write a book. Needless to say, I was shocked and amazed by the outpouring of interest. One interview had changed the course of my writing career.

As a result of the *New York Times* article, I picked up a lot of freelance writing work, and my ebook, *Smalltopia: A Practical Guide to Working for Yourself*, sold over four hundred copies during

August 2010. That probably doesn't seem like a lot of books, but I was shocked that it did so well. My initial goal was to sell fifty copies of the ebook. I'm grateful that I can do what I love for a living and honored to be writing for so many amazing readers.

I've found that success knocks on the door when I'm engaged in activities that fill me with passion. Indeed, when I think about my past, I wonder why I didn't become a writer sooner. I remember sitting in front of my dad's fireplace in Lake Tahoe as a teenager waiting for my stepmom to give me feedback on a school history paper. I was anxious for her comments, and I jotted down thoughts in my journal as I waited. When my stepmom finished reading the paper, not only did she tell me that she enjoyed it, but she encouraged me to write more often and consider majoring in liberal arts because the degree would give me more flexibility. I brushed aside her feedback because I didn't consider myself a "good writer." Instead of listening to her, I ended up majoring in economics, and I'm not even good at math! Economics was an interesting subject and challenging, but I chose it and ignored my passion for writing because I felt like a degree in economics would help me get a "good job." Also, I didn't think it would be possible to make much money as a social worker or as a writer.

Of course, following your passion isn't always easy. Writing itself can be daunting and frustrating, but I persevere, happily, because I believe passionately in the rewards it brings. As Gretchen Rubin notes in *The Happiness Project*, "Happiness doesn't always make you feel happy."

Nor does simplifying or downsizing your life always make you feel happy. For myself, going from investment management to victim advocacy and then to writing were huge, scary changes. I was only able to make these changes slowly, over time, taking one small actionable step every day.

Jolie Guillebeau: Making Deliberate Choices

As a student of happiness, I couldn't help but notice the name of the café. My friend Jolie and I decided to meet for an early morning coffee date at Happy Sparrow. It's a tiny little café in southeast Portland bursting with bright colors and smiling faces. Over breakfast, we talked about knitting, relationships, and Jolie's art.

Ever since she was a little girl, Jolie wanted to paint, but she always ran into roadblocks. Throughout elementary school, high school, and even college, she tried to enroll in art classes, but for some reason never could. Either the classes were full or instructors told her she didn't meet the requirements of the course. Instead, Jolie decided that she'd become a teacher. Yet the desire to paint never left her.

After college, Jolie started working as a high school teacher. She knew teaching was one of her gifts, yet she wasn't sure if the public school setting was the right spot for her to thrive. She felt like something was missing. She slowly started reexamining the type of work she wanted to do. After she'd been teaching for three years, her husband suggested that she take a year off to focus on painting. Jolie agreed, quit her teaching job, and resolved to take a sabbatical.

During Jolie's sabbatical, she went to art classes every day and then came home and worked on her craft for hours. She sped through the material. After three months, her teacher said, "I've taught you everything I can. You need to enroll in Jack Dempsey's courses. Try and talk with him because his classes fill up quickly. I have to warn you, he's a little cranky."

One night her husband was playing a gig at a jazz club, and Jolie happened to look over and see Jack Dempsey drinking a beer. Jolie summoned up all her courage and meandered over to him. She said, "Hi, Mr. Dempsey, my teacher suggested that I talk to you about your art course. I'm wondering if you still have room in your class?"

Jack didn't seem to have the slightest bit of interest in Jolie, but he asked to see her portfolio. Luckily, she had it with her. Jack opened it and literally put Jolie's drawings up to his nose. Then Jack looked at Jolie and said, "I think we'll get along just fine. Here's a list of things you need to purchase before class next week." Jolie was ecstatic. She told me that was "the moment" — the moment she realized that she could make a living from her art.

I asked Jolie, "Do you think your path toward a successful career has to do with living simply?"

"It's not about simplicity. I don't consider myself a minimalist. It's about making deliberate choices. You see, we've always been adamant about not having debt. Not being saddled with debt has given us the freedom to make career choices that fit our personalities and lifestyle."

"So are you happier now?"

"Yes, I'm happier. I'm much more content because I'm being true to myself. I still love teaching and I bring that into my art. But I also balance that with my own creativity."

Jolie told me the process of embracing her identity as an artist took ten years. During her sabbatical, she continued to introduce herself as a teacher. "It's all about taking small steps," Jolie said. "It wasn't until I started saying that I was an artist that I believed it. Your body has to hear you say the word before you can embrace your identity." Jolie spent nine years teaching in both public and private schools, and she still teaches, just not in a traditional setting. She teaches private art lessons from her art studio at home.

Jolie is a big believer in taking small actionable steps. For instance, instead of focusing on large paintings that might take forty hours to complete, she wanted to do something on a smaller scale. Jolie's first project after her sabbatical was called *One Hundred Paintings in One Hundred Days*. She posted her paintings on her website. It was the act of committing to the project publicly that kept her going and reignited her confidence. Since then, Jolie's done a number of other cool painting projects, including *The Summer Sunshine* series, for which she painted landscapes of Portland, as well as *100 Faces*, *100 Abstracts*, and now a series called *100 Stories*.

One of the few pieces of art in my home is by Jolie. It's a very tiny portrait of my cat Elaina. Every time I look at the painting, I'm reminded of a few important lessons. First, rethinking work is a recipe for happiness. Second, overcoming fear and doing what you love for a living isn't selfish — on the contrary, you're more likely to be engaged with the world. Finally, I remember Jolie herself. She's built a career around her art — something she's wanted to do since she was seven years old. I find that incredibly awesome.

Micro-actions

If you're not happy, changing your circumstance also means changing your attitude. In *Ruling Your World*, Sakyong Mipham notes, "The most practical way to ensure forward movement on the path of rulership is to train for a short time each day in changing our attitude — just 10 percent." We have to be open to the possibility of positive change and then actively work toward it. I overcame my fears by taking one small actionable step every day. Eventually, these small steps give us the momentum we need to make the big shifts we want — in our career or our circumstances. If it seems to happen slowly, that's okay. Living simply has taught me how important it is to let go of rigid expectations and to be open to new opportunities — and how a small shift in attitude can literally change your life.

- **Create a journal that focuses on your passion.** If you believe you can do something, passion and focus follow. Something that helped me tremendously was starting a journal and writing down all my hopes, desires, and dreams. I wrote about the things that brought me joy and happiness;

I wrote about the skills I love to use. Once I'd given voice to these things, I started making them a reality.

- **Every morning, list your three most important tasks for the day.** Usually, I write down my list with a cup of coffee in my hand and some kind of sugary treat near my computer. Focusing on three projects or tasks is a whole lot more doable than trying to do twenty things on a running to-do list.
- **Prioritize your spending.** If you're thinking of making a huge career change and quitting your day job, make sure you have a savings account. For instance, when I left my day job, I had one year of expenses saved. A financial cushion was ideal for me because it decreased my anxiety during the transition period. Don't undermine your efforts with poor financial planning. For more tips and ideas, see chapter 4.
- **Take classes and read as much as possible.** To start changing careers, read as much as possible about what you'd like to be doing and enroll in career-specific classes. This is also a great way to connect with your peers. Meeting people and developing relationships with fellow bloggers and writers are valuable sources for learning about and sustaining my passion.
- **Test the waters.** If you're thinking of starting your own business, test your target market. Start a blog, write an ebook, or develop a free online class; these are great ways to get feedback on business ideas and to find out if people are interested in the concept.
- **Be aware of your media consumption.** At one time I spent countless hours watching TV and surfing the Internet. Some mindless entertainment is fine, but ultimately our time is limited. Do you want to say you spent it watching TV?

Dedicate an hour to job searches and business research for every hour you spend on Facebook.

- **Seek out mentors and ask for help.** Ask people you admire to help you achieve your career goals. I have a few amazing mentors who helped me work up the courage to leave my day job and start writing full-time. For instance, I met with a businesswoman I admired once a week for coffee to review the status of the various goals I'd set for myself. Without help from my mentors, I wouldn't be where I am today.

PART 3

[Buying Happiness]

CHAPTER 8

Time Is the Only Real Wealth

Instead of resigning ourselves to lives in which 75 percent of the day is less enjoyable or at best, neutral, we can find ways to enliven and transform these moments.

— TODD KASHDAN

It was a cool August day in Lake Tahoe, and my mom and I were sitting on the beach reading. She was leafing through the latest issue of a real estate magazine, and I was reading a book called *Curious?* by Todd Kashdan. I turned to my mom and said, "This is incredible!"

My mom slid her sunglasses down the bridge of her nose and asked, "What's so incredible?"

"Well, according to Todd Kashdan, most people spend less than 20 percent of their day engaged in meaningful work or activities, like talking with close friends, making love, or just playing."

My mom's mouth fell open. "That's shocking! It makes me wonder if people have fun anymore."

It turns out that a number of researchers have asked the same question. For instance, in 2007, Princeton economist Alan Krueger published a fascinating paper called "Are We Having More Fun Yet?" Over the past ten years, massive technological advances should have given people a vast amount of newly free time. According to Krueger, that's not the case. Americans feel they still don't have enough time to engage in meaningful or challenging activities.

I have come to see time as a nonrenewable resource and an extremely valuable commodity. It's something we never get back. Nor can we hoard it or always count on having it. Tomorrow, our account may be bankrupt. Since that's true, we each need to evaluate how we're spending this resource. In general, I've chosen to make less money for the freedom to spend a week like the one I was having with my parents at Lake Tahoe. If I was working a traditional job, I wouldn't have been sitting on the beach with my mom, engrossed in a meaningful conversation. That said, I still work hard and struggle to find the perfect balance between work and play. My work fills me with happiness, but sometimes not working creates stress and feelings of guilt.

Interestingly, one study examined how focusing on personal time versus money influenced an individual's pursuit of happiness. Researchers found that when subjects focused on spending time with friends and family, they worked less and were happier, whereas those who focused on making more money worked more, socialized less, and were not as happy. In essence, "increased happiness requires a shift in attention toward time." I've found this to be true in my own life. Spending more time with friends and family members and starting my own business were key elements in how I viewed happiness.

As I worked to make this happen, I started tracking my time (for more about doing this, see *168 Hours* by Laura Vanderkam). It's been a very beneficial exercise that has helped me figure out how many hours of leisure time I have, how much time I spend working, and how much time I "waste." I'm much more mindful of how I spend my time now. Time is magical and I want to make the most of it.

In this chapter, I look at three areas where we often "waste" the most time: on our commutes, watching TV, and surfing the Internet.

The Thirty-Second Commute

Commuting seems to be a stress that doesn't pay off.

— Alois Stutzer and Bruno Frey

When happiness researchers ask people to talk about the worst part of their day, people consistently name commuting. In a study called "Stress That Doesn't Pay: The Commuting Paradox," Alois Stutzer and Bruno Frey found that commuting long distances to work is detrimental to our happiness and physical health. Interestingly, they found a negative connection between the amount of time spent commuting and a person's overall life satisfaction. Stutzer and Frey noted that people who drive to work would "have to earn 19 percent more per month in order to be fully compensated." Extra income is always helpful, but that doesn't solve the real problem: we spend too much time in our cars. This directly takes away from time we could be spending doing the things that make us happy.

As I've described, my daily commute was once debilitatingly long. My commute, one way, could be ninety minutes or more with traffic, and there always seemed to be traffic. All that time in my car led to constant frustrations and serious back problems — which I guess is what happens when you spend so much time, like I did, pounding the steering wheel and yelling at other drivers. On average, Americans spend about fifty minutes in their car every day, and nine out of ten trips are made by car. What can you do about it? First of all, stop commuting.

Of course, not everyone can, but it's important to see that commuting is a choice. I chose to become a self-employed writer, in part, to gain back all the time I had lost to commuting. Now my commute is stress-free and takes about thirty seconds. Since my house is so small, maybe not even that long. I climb down from the loft, sit in my window nook, open my laptop, and start writing. Now I cringe to think of all the time I used to spend in my car. In the effort to simplify your life, consider how you can eliminate or decrease your commute time. Is it worth a big home in a far-flung suburb if you're hardly ever there, and when you arrive at the end of each day, you're exhausted and frazzled? Is it worth a particular job if it drags you halfway across the state with no work-at-home options?

The other strategy is to commute by any other method than by car. If you can't avoid a commute, turn your commute into an activity that improves your well-being, rather than detracting from it. Try commuting by train, bus, or bicycle. This is what I did prior to starting my own business. Rather than drive from Davis to my job in Sacramento, I took the Amtrak train and then I walked to the office. I loved it! The train ride was short — a mere fifteen-minute ride — and even though the train was always running late, I rarely stressed out. That's because I could use the extra time to read, write, or knit — activities that enriched my time. I couldn't do any of those things when I was in my car, stuck in traffic.

If you take kids to and from school every day, consider doing so by bike or public transportation. My sister-in-law Tina (whom I introduced in chapter 7) now bikes with her kids to school and loves it. She explained, "I wouldn't have started taking Isaac and Ella to school on the bike if my husband hadn't taken my car keys by accident. It was the only way to get the kids to school. A friend of mine had recently come over for a play date, and she helped me. I had to actually put things together. It was a big step for me. The kids had a blast playing on the lawn, while I was throwing tools across the garage."

Despite the frustrating morning emergency, Tina noted, "The bike path was quiet and taking the kids to school on the bike was a peaceful experience. I also had better visibility on my bike. Overall, being in the bike trailer teaches the kids how to respect someone else's space. If you avoid teaching your kids these lessons, you push it off and it will come up later in life. I don't have a lot of opportunities to work out, so biking the kids to school is something I can do with them and get exercise, too. Ninety percent of the time they are in love with the bike and don't fight much. They get better and better. It's really about reframing how you look at things." For Tina, serendipity led to a long-lasting pleasurable habit.

My friend Dusti Arab loves commuting by bike, by herself and with her kids, because it keeps her healthy and fit. However, in the beginning it was hard. She told me, "Bike commuting as a mom sucks for the first few weeks. But keep doing it. I promise, it gets better."

Surprised, I asked, "Why does it suck?"

"I don't care how in shape you are, it will wear your body out. For the most part cycling with kids is safe. But there are some communities where that is not a reality. I've never had a problem with Evie because I have a yellow trailer, and it makes us visible. If you are well marked, you'll be okay. As far as weather goes, if you prepare, you'll be fine. We live in Oregon and it rains a lot. It's all about preparation."

When we spoke, Dusti was pregnant, and she gave birth to a baby boy, named Tristan, in early 2012. This forced her to make adjustments. Dusti said, "Before I can cycle with the baby, he has to be able to hold his head up. Until that happens, I'm going to use a sling and take him everywhere with me. We'll use public transit for at least six months, and after that period we'll probably get a front-loading bike seat for him — one that will swap out easily. Kids always look so happy in the front-loading seats."

I asked Dusti why she keeps biking with her kids. She explained that it's a lot of fun and, more importantly, the kids have fun. It's all about the experience.

My husband, Logan, considers commuting by bike one of the best parts of his day. He's been biking to work for several years, and it takes about thirty minutes to get to the office. He said, "Biking is fun, whether it's sunny or rainy. It wakes me up, gets my blood going, and parking is easy. Plus, I don't have to wait for the bus or train."

For us, changing our daily commute was one way we regained control over our time.

Why I Don't Own a TV

Today, the average American home contains more TVs than people. In 1950, only 5 percent of American homes had TVs. By 1960, over 95 percent of American homes had TVs, and that's not all. According to the Bureau of Labor Statistics, watching TV is the primary leisure activity for Americans today, the one they do the most. On average, Americans spend about 2.8 hours per day watching television; that's over a thousand hours a year!

In 2005, right before I left the investment management industry, Logan and I fell right in line with this average. At the end of a long day spent mostly sitting — in my car during my commute and in my cubicle for eight hours (or more) at work — I'd sit in front of the television for two or three more hours each night. Most of the time Logan and I would flip through the channels hoping some program would catch our eye while complaining about commercials. The longer I watched TV, the less alive I felt. I was turning into a zombie, so I proposed a change.

As I was reevaluating my leisure time, I decided to replace watching television with reading and, hopefully, doing fun things together with Logan, like taking evening walks and going for bike rides. But when I excitedly presented my plan for watching less TV, I became disheartened. Logan wasn't interested. He didn't want to give up his TV habit. We were in the process of decluttering our lives, and I suggested that we donate the TV to a friend. Logan wasn't thrilled and resisted this idea.

However, I was soon pleasantly surprised when he suggested a compromise. Around this same time, Logan volunteered to participate in a heart study at the University of California at Davis. For the study, he had to wear a heart-rate monitor throughout his day. What he discovered was that his heart rate was lower while watching TV than it was while he was sleeping. Logan felt the TV was acting like a drug that put him in a vegetative state. He reasoned that a low heart rate could be a contributor to heart disease.

Rather than give the TV away, he suggested that we put it in the closet. If it was out of sight, we wouldn't be tempted to watch it, but if we wanted or needed the TV, we could pull it out and plug it back in. For months, the TV sat in the closet, unwatched and collecting dust. In fact, one of our cats loved sleeping on top of it. We both learned that we could survive and thrive without a TV.

Recently, Logan and I talked about our fights over the TV. He said, "Well, we both agreed that we needed to downsize. I agreed to part with the TV because I knew I had to start living without so much stuff. In the back of my mind, I knew I had the computer. So if I wanted to watch a show, I could always log on to the Internet. Hiding the TV in the closet forced me to be more intentional about how I used my time. Surprisingly, I felt happier without the TV constantly blaring, and I wasn't exposed to so much advertising, which curbed my desire to buy more stuff." Logan described the TV as "a small sun in the solar system of my life. Everything seemed to center around the TV, including our furniture."

Ultimately, how you spend your time and energy is what your life becomes. Yet Logan put his finger on another big, time-related problem I had to conquer — the Internet.

My Digital Sabbatical

When I was in high school, I was scared of the Internet. I didn't have a personal computer or an Internet connection. When I had to do research for papers, I always asked my best friend's parents for help. They lived a block away and I drove over to their house to do research.

The Internet seemed like a big monster. I avoided it and email until I got to college, when I knew I'd have to get over my fear. I distinctly remember the first time I checked my email in college. All new students received free email accounts, and a few of my professors were going to send out assignments via email. I was sitting in the student union, staring at a computer screen like a dutiful student, going through the process of creating my new email account. It's hard to believe that was fifteen years ago.

I've always been a "late adopter" when it comes to technology, though today my life and work are intimately connected with it. It's funny how things change over time. All of my jobs have used computer technology and resources. During my time in investment management, I helped out with a huge database migration project. When I worked at a local rape crisis center, we built a website as an outreach tool. When I started working at California Coalition Against Sexual Assault (CALCASA), I learned all about blogging, social networking, and how the policy world worked. The work I did at CALCASA changed how I viewed technology, particularly how it can be used for good.

In September 2010, the Chartered Institute for IT released an intriguing report about Internet use and happiness. Interestingly, the results suggest that some people benefit more than others from the Internet, including those with lower incomes, people living in the developing world, and women. The researchers said the Internet has "an indirect, enabling, and empowering role leading to a greater sense of freedom and control which in turn leads to greater life satisfaction." In other words, Internet access will make you happier as long as it's used in moderation.

But is that the way most Americans use it? On my daily walks around Portland, I see more and more people staring down at glowing screens, not paying attention to their surroundings. It makes me wonder if being constantly plugged into technology is a detriment to our happiness.

A number of researchers and reporters have found that constantly scrolling through email, sending text messages, and logging on to social networks fire up the "dopamine-reward system." Sherry Turkle has written extensively about people's relationship with technology; she noted recently, "We must lead examined lives with our digital objects and constantly question what is served by always being on."

As I assessed my own time, I knew that I was plugged into my laptop and iPod way too much. I wasn't clinically "addicted" to the Internet, but I was constantly multitasking and toggling between screens. I kept asking myself questions like: Did I really need to check my email every hour? Would twice a day suffice? The more I checked my email and various social networks, the busier and less focused I felt. Even for a blogger, being constantly plugged in didn't seem to improve my productivity.

This is a common problem today. Journalist Marjorie Connelly reported in the *New York Times* that 30 percent of people under forty-five years of age said "the use of devices (like smart phones) makes it a whole lot harder to focus." In addition, juggling email, phone calls, and other incoming messages changes the way people think and behave, and not for the better. As Connelly noted, our ability to focus is being "undermined by bursts of information. These play to a primitive impulse to respond to immediate opportunities and threats."

The answer, of course, is to unplug. I started small by unplugging during weekends. For two days, I didn't turn on the computer at all for any reason. I did this for six months, and the experience was refreshing. I was reading more often on the weekends, spending quality time with Logan, and taking a lot of yoga classes. It's amazing what I can accomplish if I'm not mindlessly scrolling through my Twitter or Facebook feed.

Then I conducted a bigger experiment. I decided to take a month-long digital sabbatical in July 2011.

My main reason for doing so was to focus on writing this book. I needed to maximize my time, and to do that, I eliminated all kinds of activities from my daily schedule, such as mindless Internet surfing. For the entire month, I didn't blog, check email, or access social media; I didn't check Twitter or Facebook. However, I didn't unplug completely. I allowed myself to do book-specific research on the Internet and to send out content to members of my subscription service. The sabbatical was an intense time to focus on writing and only writing.

Even unplugging to this degree for a month made me nervous. At this point, I'd been blogging for over three and half years. I was scared that my readers would be upset and might unsubscribe from my site. On the other hand, I had a good reason to unplug. When I was constantly reacting to incoming messages, I wasn't getting work done.

During my sabbatical, I worked a lot, but I had mixed emotions and reactions. In fact, I felt like I was on an extended vacation in some ways, and I spent a lot more time outside and with friends. At times I felt happier as I let go of my need to stay "connected" and updated on everything. That said, I also missed this connection. At the start of the sabbatical I felt isolated. Instead of using email to stay connected with distant friends and family, I made more phone calls, but this wasn't the same, strangely enough. In essence, I struggled with a loneliness that was a symptom of Internet withdrawal.

Ultimately, taking a break from the digital world was refreshing and centering. The Internet and social media bring me an incredible amount of happiness. I love connecting with readers and writers and keeping up with friends and family. But if I spend too much time online, I start feeling unhappy, dissatisfied, and disconnected from the real world. Sometimes stillness and silence are the best way to harness creativity.

The idea of living simply extends to all interactions and experiences. Most of all, it's about making the most of your time. It's important to consider and manage what relationships you devote your time to. For a long time, I woke up and immediately logged on to Facebook. I wanted to check in on and connect with all my friends. But is that what I was really doing?

This question came home to me one morning as I powered up my computer and logged on to Facebook. A sea of faces popped up in my news feed, and I had fifteen new friend requests. Yet I didn't know any of these people. I'm sure they were all great folks; no doubt, they all knew somebody who knew somebody who knew me. However, it suddenly felt so out of control. I knew "Facebook friends" weren't necessarily the same types of good friends I'd call if I was feeling depressed or if I wanted to meet for coffee and an in-depth conversation. But was I even being a good digital friend anymore? As I sat in front of my computer, I realized I no longer had the capacity to be "friends" with seven hundred people, and I had to start fresh. I could barely keep up with my friends in town. Today, I have a Facebook Fan page for RowdyKittens.com, and I post updates when I add new content to the site. I don't use my personal Facebook account, so I don't have any "Facebook friends." When I want to talk with my friends, I make a phone call or write a letter.

I still struggle with balance. I'm a blogger; by definition that means I have an online presence and persona. I use email and have a Twitter account, and it's tempting to check them and respond every five minutes. However, I've been down that road, and it's counterproductive. So I've put a few rules in place. Typically, I check my email around 10 AM and then again around 3 PM, and the same goes for social networking sites. Sometimes I adjust my timeline depending on my schedule. Now I unplug every Sunday, and I recommend the practice. In a way, it's more relaxing and balancing than taking a month-long sabbatical, though that is eye-opening as well.

Then again, I've been known to fall off the wagon. When I do, I use a program called Freedom. Freedom is an application that locks you away from the Internet for up to eight hours at a time. It's ironic, perhaps, that I need my computer to restrain my own social media impulses, but maybe it's no different from sticking your TV in a closet. It's about making choices that improve the quality of your time and not letting it be filled with mindless distractions.

Micro-actions

- **Track your time for a week.** Print out a calendar and fill in the blanks as you move through your week. Make note of how much time you spend working, watching TV, commuting to and from work, surfing the Internet, exercising, and more. For example, in 2005, tracking my time — and discovering that I spent between twenty and thirty hours each week just commuting and watching TV — helped me see what I was missing and reprioritize activities that I enjoyed.

- **Write down your activities.** Writing down all your activities will help quantify the balance in your life. To increase your joy, which activities should you cut back on or eliminate, if possible? Some will be easier than others. In the time you free up, what activities can you add that increase your happiness and well-being?
- **How much time do you spend with your car?** Add up the hours you spend with your car every day. Include the time spent commuting, getting gas, dealing with maintenance issues, and looking for parking spaces. Are there ways you can decrease the amount of time you spend with your car? Can you carpool, take more public transit, or join a car-sharing program?
- **Do a test run and park it.** Not sure you can go car-free or car-lite? Test it out for a week or a month. Find out exactly how much this change will affect your life as you go through everyday tasks. Then weigh any inconvenience against the money you'll save if you sell your car.
- **Give yourself thirty days.** Researchers note that incorporating any kind of new habit into your life requires between twenty-one and thirty days. If you're trying to kick an obsessive habit, like checking email every half hour, start small and persist for at least a month.
- **Change your work flow by single-tasking.** Multitasking erodes my mental circuitry. Now I focus on single-tasking. Practice doing one thing till it's finished, and eliminate all distractions till it's done.

CHAPTER 9

Money vs. Experiences

Life shouldn't be printed on dollar bills.

— Clifford Odets

On July 12, 2010, as I loaded up my panniers — bike bags that can be clipped onto a bike rack — I started to worry. Was it wise for our first bike camping trip to be a forty-mile ride from Portland to Stub Stewart State Park? Before we decided to take this trip, Logan and I had some heated conversations about bike camping. I didn't think I could handle the mileage. However, Logan assured me I was in good-enough shape.

It turned out my anxiety was warranted. That day was one of the hottest days of the summer, and by the time we got to Banks, Oregon, we were both exhausted. At one point, Logan left me in the shade by a Safeway to pick up my favorite drink — lemon-flavored Gatorade. The sweet, salty drink never tasted so good, and I needed it. We still had ten more miles to ride to reach the campground.

Eventually, Logan and I made it to the park. For me, those final ten miles were brutal. However, once we'd recovered, we had one of the best weekends of the summer, and for fifty dollars, I'd say it was cost-effective. The cost of the trip included our campsite, food, and a few bottles of beer. Could Logan and I have spent the weekend in a pretty bed-and-breakfast if we'd wanted? Certainly, and we probably wouldn't have had as much fun. For one thing, the experience taught me that I'm stronger than I think, and memories like these are more important and lasting than any object I could buy.

Seven years ago, I would have shunned bike camping because it wasn't "cool." I would have been worried about messing up my hair or getting dirty. Now, I'm happy to head out for a bike camping trip. The times I spend with Logan exploring the natural world are experiences that bring me joy.

As Scott Russell Sanders noted in an article entitled "Breaking the Spell of Money": "Beyond meeting our basic needs, money cannot give us any of the things that actually bring happiness — family, community, good health, good work, experience of art and nature, service to others, a sense of purpose, and spiritual insight."

To break my own spell around money I've become very intentional about whom I choose to spend my time with and the type of stuff I buy.

My Mom, Kathy Hettick: Money Buys Stability, Not Happiness

I introduced my mom, Kathy Hettick, in chapter 1, and I want to share a little bit more of her story, since it's informed many of my life choices. If I'm skeptical of the connection between money and happiness, that you need one to buy the other, it's in part because of my mom's experiences and perspective.

After my mom finished college, she decided to leave New York and move to San Francisco. She explained, "I needed to get away from my mom, your grandmother, Mary Jane. She was so strict and hard on me, even at the age of twenty-one. There were a lot of compounding factors, and I had to go live my own life. So I moved to San Francisco and started working as an executive secretary."

When my mom moved to the city, she found a small apartment at the YMCA. At the time, they had small studios for rent in San Francisco, and since she was starting fresh, it was the perfect spot for her to land. She didn't have any furniture, but she had a new job and was excited to start exploring the city. Her apartment was about three hundred square feet, which propelled her to get outside more often. My mom noted, "It was comfortable and small, and I had a PO box for my mail. Then I rented an apartment with a friend for a few years. It was out in the avenues, around 45th and Rivera."

She said, "I lived a lot like you guys. My only care in the world was my first bicycle. I bought it in downtown San Francisco at Macy's. Besides my bike, the only other thing I really valued was my skis. I was about twenty-one or twenty-two and my apartment was near a high-class shopping, restaurant, and bar area. One of my favorite hangouts was the Hudson Bay Inn. I would ride my bike down to the inn, have a glass of wine at the bar, and flirt with the boys.

"I adapted to city life. It was three years before I could afford to fly home. On my first trip back, Dad helped me with the cost of the plane ticket. I never asked for money. They had a lot, but I just didn't ask. At the time I was a secretary, and back in those days I was able to save money and pay my rent. Dad was always impressed by that and something he remembered about me; I didn't beg for money."

My mom lived a very comfortable life in the city. However, her financial situation changed drastically in her early thirties. She received an inheritance of $250,000 from her uncle Bill a few years before I was born (in 1978). Five years after I was born, my parents divorced. My mom remarried (to my stepdad Mahlon) when I was in high school. I was extremely lucky growing up; my parents had plenty of money. We didn't want for clothes or food, and we lived in a beautiful ranch-style home. Plus we had enough disposable income to go on skiing trips and other vacations.

When I asked my mom if she thought money could buy happiness, she said, "Money can't buy happiness, but it can provide financial stability. After the divorce from your dad, I don't know where we would have ended up without the inheritance. I know I was very fortunate to have financial assets." Interestingly, she said she's certain that if the inheritance hadn't appeared, she would have worked something out. "I believe happiness comes from the inside. Sure, the money gave us a better quality of life. However, you don't have to inherit money to be wealthy in spirit."

Uncle Bill himself was an example. She said, "Uncle Bill was so unhappy. He literally drank himself to death. He had everything he could want — women, cars, and a big house. Yet he wasn't happy. Even my parents fought about money constantly, and we had plenty. All the late-night arguments were about money. The problems always came back to money."

As an adult, my mom never strove to be "rich" because she never wanted to be like her uncle Bill. She told me that money is nice and it can provide comfort, but it depends on how you use it. She said, "The question is, do you spend money on cars, homes, and drugs, like famous people, or do you use it for your future financial security and donate to causes you believe in?" Throughout my mom's life she has wanted only enough money to feel secure, and she's grateful for the experiences she had as a kid. She got to attend summer camp — something that most of her friends didn't experience — and she has gone on extended ski trips throughout her life. Skiing is an activity she adores.

Like many Americans, my mom lost a huge chunk of her inheritance in the 2008 stock market crash. Sometimes she wishes she had more money, but overall she's happy despite the challenges she's facing right now. She recently told me, "I'd rather be broke and have my health. With good health you can do anything you want." As she emphasized, the most important thing a strong body and mind provide is the ability to focus on enjoying your life and relishing experiences.

Distinguishing Needs from Wants

Elizabeth W. Dunn, an associate professor at the University of British Columbia, is at the forefront of research on consumption and happiness. In recent papers, Dunn and her colleagues explained that income is not a strong predictor of happiness once our basic needs are met. The studies they reviewed suggested that money can buy happiness, but it depends on how you spend your disposable income.

The question is: When you purchase something, how long does the happiness last compared to the money you spend? For example, if you buy the perfect Gucci bag and are longing for another one within a week, then you've received only a temporary happiness boost. Humans adapt very rapidly to new things in their lives, so the happiness from "newness" wears off quickly. However, spending money on experiences — concert tickets, taking a yoga class, or going on vacation — typically produces more, and longer lasting, satisfaction than buying stuff because we're impacting our well-being, and joyful memories continue to feed us. Instead of buying stuff, Dunn and her colleagues show that you can be happier by helping others, donating to charities, and buying a few small pleasures.

My friend Dusti Arab exemplifies these research findings. Dusti is a twenty-three-year-old writer and full-time mom whom you met in chapter 8. She's also a savvy businesswoman who recently downsized her life. I interviewed Dusti at a local Portland coffee and chocolate shop called Moonstruck in late 2011. If you haven't noticed, coffee and sugar are two of my biggest weaknesses.

During our conversation she noted, "Before simplifying, the only concept of happiness I had was based on stuff. Happiness was Disneyland. It was what Disney sells. Once you strip away excess stuff, there's no way to avoid the rest. Prior to last year, I had no grasp on what my value system was. I couldn't articulate how I felt about an issue. Simplifying was my first step toward self-actualization. It started with stuff, then I looked at how I was spending my time and asked myself: 'What do I actually want to do with my time? My life?' It took me a full year to figure that out, and it's only been within the past month that I've developed my mission and purpose. When stuff isn't in the way, you have to think about the aspects of your life that are making you unhappy."

Dusti knows what she wants to teach her children. She explained, "Experiences are the priority; that's what I want to give my kids. Experiences will fulfill their lives, and they will have happy memories to draw on as adults." Her comment reminded me of my own childhood; for the most part my mom, dad, and stepfather constantly emphasized the importance of life experiences.

Dusti went on to explain, "Money can buy happiness up to a certain point. I come from a background where I lived under the poverty line my whole life, and this is the first year I've gotten above that line. I believe a family can live happily on thirty thousand dollars a year, and that is pretty much true for me. When I start making thirty-five thousand dollars a year, we can put the rest into savings. As far as money and happiness go, money is useful in that it can buy experiences. You can invest in education and better yourself, and you can donate to causes you believe in."

When I asked my blog readers about experiences versus money, they had a lot to say about the importance of helping others, achieving personal goals, and buying experiences. Here are a few of their responses:

> Money in and of itself cannot buy happiness. We just went through the most stressful months of our married lives due to unemployment and underemployment. It was the first time in our twenty-four-year marriage that we really didn't have the money to buy nearly anything we wanted (or to take out a loan for it). Although we were stressed, it didn't rock our core — the love and happiness we share together.

> Money doesn't buy happiness but reducing debt and getting smart about money frees us from an economic trap. If we choose wisely, we can live a more stress-free life, which in turn leads to increasing happiness. So it's not money that directly buys freedom and happiness but our choice about how we choose to live.

> From personal experience, money doesn't buy happiness past a certain threshold. Meaning, once you can live comfortably (whatever that means to you) and do what you want (again, your definition), then striving for more digits in the bank account won't do anything. Earning $100k vs $20k? Yes, big difference. Earning $200k vs $100k? Not so much of a life change anymore. Experiences are where happiness truly lives. For example, a one-way plane ticket to a far-off land and the resulting experiences that come from that. You need a certain amount of money to have that experience.

Ultimately, what "simplifying your life" means to me is structuring your life based on your values. As the last quote above says, you have to define what this means for yourself. This is why I like Dee Williams's comment that living in a tiny house is about "smart-sizing" yourself rather than "downsizing." By living in a tiny house, I've let go of what I don't need, so that my life feels full and satisfying in the ways I prefer, in the ways that create the least stress and the most happiness for me.

To do this, I had to question my values and become more intentional about the lifestyle I created. I discovered that the power of my intentions was key in my happiness equation. When I had a big apartment and two cars, the overall focus of my life became paying for those possessions. As a result, I spent a lot of hours working in a job I didn't enjoy to earn money to pay for my stuff. Yet when I examined my values more closely, I saw that I didn't really "need" these things. I had lost track of the core lessons my parents taught me as a kid. What I really wanted was to be able to focus on my relationships and community, but I couldn't because I was too busy paying for a lifestyle I couldn't afford, and that ruined my quality of life.

This is the happiness equation to use, then, when distinguishing needs from wants. The question isn't "What do I need to support my current lifestyle?" The question is "What do I want most out of life, and what lifestyle supports that best?" What do you value, and how do you build a life that supports those values? For myself, I valued relationships, community, and experiences. By living in a tiny house and having fewer material goods, I created a lifestyle free from debt that gives me the freedom to pursue these things.

What is the happiness equation in your life? Does your lifestyle support your values? As Dusti says, it's easy to accept culturally defined yet faulty ideas of "happiness" that are based on acquiring material wealth. Yet everyone has different perspectives and circumstances. The lifestyle you choose will be unlike mine, or Dusti's, or my mom's. Even though their lives aren't similar, Dusti and my mom have both made intentional choices in order to "smart-size" themselves. Dusti lives with her kids and partner in an 800-square-foot apartment just outside Portland. Since they want to be closer to downtown, they are looking for a smaller, cheaper place that ranges between 500- and 700-square feet, whereas my mom lives in a 2,000-square-foot house and is focused on decluttering her possessions and her life.

Ultimately, "simplifying your life" means being open, vulnerable, and courageous enough to redefine the way you live — because you want to. Prior to 2007, I had never heard of tiny homes, and I would never have imagined or considered living in one. That changed thanks to YouTube and Dee Williams. She showed me how to buy the kind of happiness I wanted. For us, our very small house provides us with the necessary resources and time to engage in the experiences that bring a profound sense of joy to my life.

Micro-actions

- **Make a list of your priorities, needs, and wants.** What do you want to spend your money on? Make a list of how you want to prioritize spending your income. What do you really need versus what do you want? Ultimately, you'll have to decide what you want to spend your time working for, which is why you have to make a list of your priorities.
- **Create a bucket list.** A "bucket list" is a list of all the things you want to do before you die. This is one way to clarify your priorities in life. How "expensive" is this list? How can you change your life to achieve these things? How many of those things involve buying more stuff? Of these "purchases," what kind of emotional experience do they embody? Is there a way to get that same emotional reward without buying another object?
- **Help others using your unique skills and abilities.** Before I started doing volunteer work, I sat down and made a list

of all the skills that I loved using, and how I could use those skills to help people in my community and in my career. Volunteering is one way I experience the world, and it grounds me. Donating money is a good thing, but volunteering directly is always much more satisfying.

CHAPTER 10

Relationships Matter, Not Things

You validate people's lives by your attention.

— UNKNOWN

My great-aunt Mamie used to collect little toys in Cracker Jack boxes. She put the toys in a small red box, and as a little girl I would come over and ask for this very tiny, yet special box. Every time I opened the box, I was filled with awe and amazement. The box overflowed with tiny toys, like Disney figurines, miniature bikes, and a very tiny Santa. I loved the little toys, but more than anything I loved spending time with my aunt. She had beautiful blue eyes and a big smile, and she always listened to me.

My aunt taught me that the key to real, long-lasting happiness is to develop good relationships. Recent research backs up this concept. For example, studies have suggested that developing strong social relationships will make us happier and healthier, and people who are happier and healthier live longer. Very happy people tend to be social and have stronger romantic and nonromantic relationships than less-happy groups.

Relationships can't be overlooked, because they surround us every moment of every day. Healthy relationships with ourselves, our spouse, our family, and our community provide a foundation to grow, improve, and prosper. Research shows that couples who have successful partnerships spend five or more hours a week talking and hanging out together.

How Living Simply Improved My Marriage

In July 2011, Logan and I celebrated our eight-year wedding anniversary. It's amazing to think of how long we've been together and of how far we've traveled since we first met — in a bar, the weekend after Valentine's Day in 2001.

My good friend Sera had to convince me to go out that night. The sky was clear and the air was cold and crisp, the perfect night to be at the Bear on its open, outdoor patio. The Bear was the hip place to hang out when I was a student at California State University at Chico. The pub was affordable, casual, and great for people watching. They had regular fun events. My favorite was the tiny trike race, where very drunk adults did laps around the lower-level bar on kid-size tricycles.

I remember the exact moment I saw Logan. He was standing behind my friend Dave, and he had a black cowboy hat, a worn brown leather coat, and big, bright-blue eyes. Within ten minutes, Logan and I were engrossed in conversation, and ever since that night we have been inseparable. Up to that moment, I always said I had bad luck when it came to love, and I never imagined that I would get married, least of all that I'd be first among all of my college friends to find a life partner.

Looking back, it's even harder to fathom, because I was the "old Tammy," the woman who was a fan of big diamonds and shopping.

I've changed and grown a great deal over the past eleven years, during which I've come to value relationships more than things and have striven to remake my life in order to improve my relationships. The first and most important has been my relationship with Logan. We pursued living more simply as a way to improve our marriage, to make sure our lives and livelihoods supported our relationship. We had to learn how to do this together; sometimes Logan pushed me, and sometimes I took the lead. Sometimes we focused on making big changes — like building and buying our tiny house — and sometimes on small ones. On the largest level, eliminating our debt and creating a life that wasn't focused on making more and more money have directly improved our marriage. Part of doing this successfully is that we stopped worrying about whether our life conformed to what other people thought we should be doing with our lives. We have done what we wanted, what makes us happy, and that involves creating lots of time together: to talk, cycle, hike, and drink coffee.

We both love coffee; it's an important morning ritual for both of us. However, in our studio apartment, while we'd drink coffee together, we were always glued to our computer screens reading blogs or books. Instead of talking we tended to zone out in the common space. After we moved into our tiny house, we decided to change that routine. Now we get up between six and seven in the morning, climb down the loft ladder, make coffee on our stove (which looks like an Easy-Bake Oven, except it's silver, not pink), and have a morning coffee date. We focus on each other, just *being* present in our tiny home together with no distractions. We didn't need our tiny house to make this change, but it helps and it's part of the same effort. And even though our morning coffee date is a relatively new routine, it's now essential to my happiness.

As Logan and I have grown together as a couple, we've realized that our physical space shapes our communication patterns. When we lived in our large 1,200-square-foot apartment in Davis, we were more likely to retreat toward separate areas of the apartment if we felt angry with each other. As we've moved into smaller and smaller dwellings, we've been less likely to run from our problems. Instead we actively communicate and resolve issues before they develop into resentment.

Simplifying has also removed the sources for most of our major conflicts: money, debt, and stuff. Selling our cars was one of the best things we ever did because it enabled us to pay off our debt. With the stress of debt removed, we don't fight as much or argue over money. Even small annoyances have disappeared: you can't argue over who didn't vacuum the carpet when you don't have a carpet. Instead of spending an entire weekend cleaning our home, we spend more time having fun together.

One worry about moving into our tiny house was that we might not have enough solitude, but this hasn't been an issue. When I need more "space," I go on a long walk and leave Logan home alone. Conversely, he will go for long bike rides on his own. Even when we're both home, if one of us reads in the loft and the other hangs out in the reading nook, we have all the personal space we need.

Another major reason for us to live small and simply has been to support each other's career goals. Resolving our money worries was essential for this. Without changing our lives the way we have, Logan wouldn't have been able to finish his PhD while I simultaneously quit my day job and started a writing business. That we can both pursue our career goals at the same time has made a big difference in the quality of our relationship. As Logan noted, "It makes us more passionate about life and it's less draining if we pursue the things we want to do. And we're happier people. It's made our relationship more cooperative instead of antagonistic."

Nurturing our relationships is essential to our happiness, but sometimes material possessions and lifestyle can actually get in the way of this. In your current life, do you have time for the activities and shared experiences that allow you to enjoy and celebrate your relationships with your spouse, friends, and family members? My morning coffee date and daily cycling trips with Logan don't appear in any GDP metric, but I guarantee our time together has helped me become a productive writer, a more engaged community member, and a better friend and daughter.

Dusti Arab: Overcoming Societal Expectations

My friend Dusti decided to start simplifying her life in early 2010, when she did both the 100 Thing Challenge and Courtney Carver's Project 333. She was excited when she successfully pared down her clothes till she could fit everything into two big suitcases. "If you put them on a plane," she said, "you'd have to pay an oversized luggage fee, but they would fit."

I laughed and asked if her partner, Andrew, resisted these changes.

"I made it a point not to touch his things in the beginning." However, once Dusti started living with less stuff, this became more appealing to Andrew. He began to embrace the idea of simplifying for himself, and it improved their relationship, too. Dusti noted, "It really gave us the time and space to focus on each other and the babies. Before, things were a mess, hard to keep track of, and it all just increased stress levels. Now, we know having less stuff has a direct correlation with the amount of time and patience we have with each other because our environment is so much nicer."

"What about your daughter, Evie?" I asked.

"I went through Evie's stuff soon after mine, and that's when the backlash started." Dusti noted that a lot of her family members didn't understand why she was getting rid of toys and other baby items, and they weren't very supportive. She said, "As an infant, she had way more clothes and baby toys — all of it gifts — than any kid needs. I began trading out toys and other things until she had just under one hundred things."

I asked, "Since I don't have kids, I get a lot of emails from folks who say, 'Well, you wouldn't understand because you don't have kids.' However, people like you have managed to downsize with kids. Do you think it's unrealistic to pare down if people have kids?"

With a slight grin Dusti said, "Do you want an honest answer?"

"Of course!" I exclaimed.

"I think it's bullshit. It's fear talking; fear of societal expectations and a possible backlash from friends and family. There are a lot of expectations when you get pregnant. As soon as you walk into the doctor's office for the first time, you're inundated with stuff — diaper bags, formulas, and free magazines, too — but 90 percent of these free things are ads or high-pressure sales articles that either push products or essentially tell parents there is only one way to raise a baby."

Dusti was expecting her second baby when we talked, and she said, "I've set up a bank account for the baby, and when I send out announcements after the birth, I'm going to encourage friends and family to give money to the baby."

"Do you think your family will support your decision?"

"No. They will just give me more stuff. I think friends will support the decision because they know I'll just donate excess stuff to Goodwill. I'm not afraid of stepping on toes anymore. My family has this idea that I don't want help, but they can't see that I'm trying to be socially conscious. I don't need more stuff."

I smiled and said, "What tips would you give parents who want to downsize more slowly and avoid family drama at the same time?"

"It's been really interesting watching my friend downsize. She's a rockin' mama, with four kids, and it's taken her about a year to downsize. She's done things in an effective way for someone who is more soft-spoken. Her parents are traditional and keep giving her gifts, but she's reframed things. When the kids get a gift, the gift stays at Grandma's house, and that's what I've done with my mom, too. I try and encourage gifts like consumables and clothing that's a size larger because kids outgrow clothes so fast, especially in the beginning. As they get older, it's harder. You can incentivize minimalism."

Dusti's story raises an important issue, which is that downsizing doesn't happen in a vacuum. When you make a major life change, it will affect your friends and family. For instance, at first, my mom and my stepdad thought our downsizing ideas were crazy, and they were worried about us, too. They worried we wouldn't be able to get to the grocery store without a car, and that Logan and I would fight more often if we moved into a small house. As we simplified we learned how important it was to communicate with my parents, to let them know we weren't crazy and to avoid hurting their feelings.

But as Dusti describes, not all of your friends and family members may understand or agree with your reasons for downsizing. Parents and extended family members may even regard radical downsizing as a criticism of one's upbringing. This isn't so surprising when you consider that one main purpose of downsizing is to question our sometimes unthinking consumptive habits and to discover and live by our own self-defined values. If downsizing causes this sort of tension among family and friends, you might consider proceeding more slowly or adjusting your efforts in different ways (for different people). For me, I pursued simplifying my life as a way to better care for and honor my most important relationships, not for it to become the source of more division.

Talking with my parents helped tremendously. Eventually, they understood that living simply would help us become debt-free and have the freedom and flexibility to pursue our dreams and have more time for family, too. Obviously, when it comes to those you live with, the effort to simplify can itself become a source of conflict if everyone doesn't agree to it. It's important to be respectful and find consensus with your partner and children; families come in all shapes and sizes, and what works in one family may not work in another. The point isn't to downsize as dramatically as possible, but to do so in ways that improve and enhance your home life and relationships.

I learned this firsthand with my stepdad, Mahlon, who loves woodworking. He would spend hours in the garage making all kinds of stuff, like Adirondack chairs, bookshelves, and more. After we got married he made us a wine rack for our apartment in Davis, and my mom painted cute little grape leaves along the sides. It was a really beautiful way to show off wine bottles. However, we gave away the wine rack after our move to Sacramento. We weren't drinking as much, and the wine rack was collecting dust and mostly empty, and it had become one more object that made our tiny apartment feel cramped. We figured it should go to a home where it would be used. However, a few months later my mom told me I'd hurt my stepdad's feelings. He was sad we gave away the wine rack, and I still feel bad about it. I don't like hurting my loved ones' feelings, and I could have avoided it, or made it less painful, by explaining my reasoning more clearly, especially since my parents have been so supportive.

Tell Me a Story

After Christmas in 2011, I visited my parents in Red Bluff, California, which is a little town filled with cowboys and spectacular sunsets. I grew up in this tiny town, and it's always nice coming home.

One night we drove down to Corning to the Rolling Hills Casino. My parents love the buffet and doing a little bit of gambling. In fact, Mahlon used to live in Reno and gambled so much that he had a line of credit at Harrah's. He told me, "During that time, I lost a lot of money and made a lot, too."

I'm not a big gambler, but I had fun following my mom around the casino taking photos and watching Mahlon at the blackjack table.

As I drove back to the house, I said, "Someone tell me a story! I'm sleepy."

Mahlon chose one of his favorite memories. It was a fun story about Roger, an old friend of his who had just died of cancer.

Mahlon grinned as he spoke: "Roger and I met in the fifth grade and became fast friends. At the time we both lived in Lodi, and it was a pretty religious community. And the town father — the priest — decided to move the Halloween festivities from Sunday to Saturday. So all of the kids were supposed to go trick-or-treating on Saturday. We went trick-or-treating on Saturday night and thought of a bright idea. We decided to go again on Sunday night and pretend we didn't know anything about the change."

"So did your trick work?" I asked.

Mahlon started laughing. "Yup. We went door-to-door again on Sunday night asking for candy and ended up getting money instead. Most of the neighbors had given their candy away, so they gave us cash! They would ask, 'Didn't you know about the date change?'

"And we would say, 'Ohhh, no. We didn't hear about that.'"

I laughed along with my dad, and he went on to tell me stories about drag racing in high school and parties out in the country. Hearing the stories of his youth made me smile.

In November 2011, Mahlon was diagnosed with Parkinson's disease, and my friend Courtney suggested that I pull a book of stories together about Mahlon's life. So over the 2011 holiday I kept asking Mahlon to tell me stories. Even though he would always protest, "I'm not good at telling stories," he'd go on to share something funny or beautiful.

When it comes to our own life, we're all good storytellers and have amazing stories to tell. But how often do we take the time to really listen and be present for one another? I know for a long time I didn't, and today I'm able to hear things that weren't on my radar in 2005. Again, simplifying my life isn't what allowed me to listen better, but it's part of how I've shifted my attention. I'm more focused on seeing and honoring others, along with their stories. More than anything, I'm thankful that I had the chance to spend quality time with my mom and Mahlon in 2011, not just over Christmas but throughout the year. And I'm thankful that I made the time to ask Mahlon to tell his stories because on January 14, 2012, everything changed for him, and for me.

Life Can Change in an Instant

It was 7:30 on Saturday morning. I had planned on getting up early, but it was rainy and cold outside and I stayed under the covers in our sleeping loft, dozing. That's where I was when my mom called. Before I picked up the phone, I immediately knew something was wrong.

My mom said, "Mahlon had a stroke this morning. He had to be airlifted to the hospital in Chico."

"No. No. No," I said, my voice shaking.

Sounding like she was still in shock, my mom explained everything that had happened just an hour before. She awoke around 6:30 AM to find Mahlon on the floor and unresponsive. She called 911 immediately, and within half an hour, first a fire truck, then an ambulance, and finally a helicopter arrived to get Mahlon to the hospital as quickly as possible.

This was Mahlon's first major stroke, and I immediately took the train home to be with my family. But even after seven weeks in an acute rehabilitation center, my dad was unable to walk or eat by himself, or to see well, and his cognitive abilities were impaired. At this point, it was clear he needed the constant supervision of a long-term care facility, but there were none in their region of Northern California that would accept him. So instead, my mom decided to bring him home and to hire in-house caregivers to help with his rehabilitation. This is where he is today, and our hope is that the familiarity of home, and the opportunity to get proper rest, will heal his brain.

It has been so difficult watching this process unfold. Witnessing a loved one's suffering is incredibly painful. All I can do is appreciate the good times and cry when I need to. As Robert Leleux said in *The Living End*, "as long as you're alive anything is possible. That sounds almost unbearably Pollyannaish, I know. It's embarrassing even to write it. But I'm not striving for optimism here. What I mean is that since life has an agonizing tendency to offer us the best and the worst at the same time, to give us what we ask for in an utterly unforeseen form, even fairly predictable outcomes prove unrecognizable upon arrival."

Events like this put everything in perspective. As we go about our daily lives, enjoying the good and coping with the bad, what are we working for? We should be treasuring our time with each other, listening and sharing more of our beautiful stories, because the time will come when we can't tell them anymore. I love the life I've created, and I'm thankful that it allows me time to be with my mom and help with the caregiving of my dad. This is what truly matters, prioritizing relationships, because life can change in an instant.

Micro-actions

In a way, most of the micro-actions in this book are meant to help you shift your focus from things and money to relationships. For example, getting my finances under control decreased my stress and allowed me to be more emotionally available. Changing my job and rethinking my daily routines gave me the time and flexibility to prioritize my relationships. With that being said, two specific common-sense actions helped me nurture my relationships as I've simplified my life.

- **Actively communicate.** If family members, friends, or your spouse doesn't understand why you want to live with less stuff, talk to them. Talking about your decisions will help your loved ones understand why you've made certain choices.
- **Make a list of activities you love and engage in those activities with loved ones.** I highly recommend making a list of activities you like to do with your partner and family. Maybe it's hiking, biking, walking, or having a conversation over coffee. The important thing is to make time for, and not neglect, your loved ones. Remember, life can change in an instant.

CHAPTER 11

The Art of Community Building

Maybe the key to happiness is to focus
less on making moments last
and more on making them count.

— LORI DESCHENE

Bookshelves, lamps, a homemade meditation cushion, an original *Star Wars* soundtrack anthology (which included Ewoks singing the Yub Yub song), a Cannon camera, a mini accordion that "was great for making joyful noises," shoe racks, patio furniture, a small propane grill, a "bazillion plastic coat-hangers," a set of fifteen plastic Godzilla miniature figurines from Japan, a refurbished Riccar vacuum cleaner: these were just some of the many belongings Lindsey Hoffman gave away during her downsizing process. Her list was full of oddball stuff and cool collections that I personally would have found hard to part with, if I'd ever owned such cool stuff in the first place.

Over dinner, Lindsey talked to me about her downsizing process, which was sparked by her desire to take an epic, yearlong road trip to visit intentional communities throughout the United States. However, her first stab at downsizing occurred when she attempted the 100 Thing Challenge.

Lindsey noted, "I was excited by the challenge because I was staying with family in Hawaii at the time, and I didn't need a lot of stuff. I tried to make a list of all the stuff I had back home, and I was surprised because I couldn't remember what I had! I knew I could live with less. But I didn't start seriously downsizing until February of 2010, when I decided to go on this trip."

Lindsey explained the reason for her trip, saying, "I was looking for a change. I had achieved the life I had striven for. I had a career, a comfortable income, and a house in a neighborhood I liked. I was living a life that I thought I wanted, yet it wasn't making me happy. Then I read a book called *The Irresistible Revolution* by Shane Claiborne. There is a chapter in which he talks about intentional communities, and I wanted to see what that would look like in action. I thought community was what I was missing in my life. I was missing 'my team.'"

You don't need to join a commune to be part of a community. An "intentional community" is nothing more than like-minded people organizing themselves around a common purpose. For example, Logan and I are part of many communities, both formal and informal. A few such intentional communities are fellow cyclists, writers, and folks who live in little homes. These communities have given us many things, including friendship and encouragement. When we first began to rethink our lifestyle, the support they provided was key. Like Lindsey, I've learned that happiness is intimately intertwined with the community you surround yourself with because everyone needs to feel like they are part of a team.

After dinner and dessert, we were sipping our tea and Lindsey remarked, "A lot of the stuff I had tied me to the past in a way that wasn't beneficial. Even though there are a lot of good memories associated with my stuff, I don't need to keep physical reminders of those memories. I feel free to move forward, and it eases my mind. I'm curious to see where this is going to end. It's like peeling an onion. The more layers I peel off, the more I can take away."

Lindsey does not know where her trip will lead. She plans to be gone for one year and to visit as many places as her time allows. Of downsizing, Lindsay said, "I'm happier because the more I give away the lighter I feel." She is preparing to go on a pilgrimage, seeking one of the most important things we can find, a community that fits us.

Finding and Defining Our Intentional Community

Logan and I started the process of simplifying in Davis, California, then moved to Sacramento, and finally to Portland, Oregon. At first I thought that simply moving to a new city would make us happier. It didn't. Plus, each time we moved, we had to make new friends and build a new community, and this took work. Yet with each move, we got better at intentionally creating a community that served and supported us.

The choice to move from Davis to Sacramento wasn't easy. We'd lived in Davis for three years and were comfortable: we loved the bike lanes, the parks, our fun local grocery cooperative, and our proximity to Amtrak. I was a member of a swim team and enjoyed bicycling the area's open country roads.

We decided to move to Sacramento as part of our downsizing process. I wanted to either walk or ride my bike to work, and moving into a small 400-square-foot apartment would enable us to shed more stuff. Plus, we had a lot of debt, and in Sacramento, our rent would be lower, allowing us to pay off our debt a little faster. We were both scared of moving to the big city because we grew up in small towns and weren't sure if we would be happy. Yet the idea of changing our living situation was enticing. Moving to Sacramento didn't mean we would find what we were looking for, but we figured we'd give it a try.

Pushing through our fear and embracing the move was a good decision. We moved to midtown Sacramento, and I was only a mile away from my office. The apartment complex reminded me of a Spanish-style building; the exterior was painted a light peach color, and it had a small courtyard, where we gathered for barbeques. Looking back, I realize it was one of the best apartment complexes I've ever lived in, and that's all because of our friendly neighbors.

However, we never would have known how friendly they were if Logan and I hadn't made deliberate efforts to meet them. Most of the time, we only "know" our neighbors on a superficial level. To really get to know someone takes time, and we aren't always willing to give that kind of time or make that effort. Upon reflection, community was abundant in Davis — we just didn't make the time to get involved. Whereas when we lived in Sacramento, we knew we had to actively create a community of new friends. We hosted frequent parties, had dinners with our neighbors, and went on lots of bike rides together, too. It was a blast!

The sense of belonging we felt was heightened once we sold our remaining car. Logan and I plugged into the Sacramento biking community and started going on group bike rides on the weekends. In addition, Logan started doing bicycle maintenance at the Sacramento Bicycle Kitchen — an organization that shares bike tools and helps people repair their bikes.

Within the first six months of 2008, we had come to love Sacramento — we had a thriving network of friends and a strong sense of belonging. Despite all that, we continued to discuss how to simplify our life further, and we became intrigued by the idea of living in a little house. Eventually, we talked about moving again, to Portland. We had dreamed of moving to the Pacific Northwest for years. The weather was perfect, the cycling culture was strong, and there was an existing network of people who lived in little houses.

As when we lived in Davis, staying in Sacramento was tempting because it was comfortable, and we were only a few hours from family. Plus, I had a good job, as a victim advocate at CALCASA, and a community I could count on. Yet the idea of moving to Portland kept emerging in our conversations. By late 2008, I'd been blogging for one year. Then, after attending the little house construction workshop in 2009, we decided to move to Portland and have Dee and Katy build our little house.

I knew that if we stayed in Sacramento, I'd never start a business around my writing. It would be too easy to hang on to my comfortable day job. I had health benefits, my salary was excellent, and it was hard to give up those kinds of perks.

Starting my own business and uprooting, yet again, would challenge me in ways that were both beneficial and emotionally difficult. I had to get active, not only in my professional life, but in my new community, too.

Putting Intentions into Action

I learned about the Portland-based organization Living Yoga before leaving Sacramento. Living Yoga is a nonprofit program that teaches "yoga as a tool for personal change to disadvantaged individuals in prisons, drug and alcohol rehabilitation centers, and facilities." I immediately knew that I wanted to volunteer with the organization in some capacity. This was the kind of community I wanted to be part of.

In February 2010, right after the move to Portland, I contacted Living Yoga's volunteer coordinator, Nancy, and asked how I could help out. Nancy said, "Well, we don't need any teachers. But we always need help in the office. Why don't you come in and we can chat." Throughout 2010 and 2011, I volunteered in the Living Yoga office. Getting active and plugging into a local network of like-minded people eased my anxiety as I settled into Portland.

For years, I made excuses for not volunteering. I never seemed to have enough time. Yet I had enough time to watch television and surf the Internet after work, and those activities always left me feeling drained. I already knew that helping other people always made me feel better, and with moving to Portland and working from home, I knew I'd need to find or create a new support system. Volunteering became an obvious solution to avoid feeling isolated and to give me a sense of purpose. Building community isn't rocket science. All it requires is dedication and effort. According to a Hindu proverb, "True happiness consists in making others happy."

The staff members at Living Yoga connected me to a lot of like-minded people, and as a result I made a lot of friends. Volunteering at Living Yoga cultivated those warm, fuzzy feelings anyone gets when they help others.

Stephen Post is the director of the Institute for Research on Unlimited Love, a group that focuses on the scientific study of service, compassion, and altruism. In a recent report called "It's Good to Be Good," he examined more than thirty different studies that focused on the health benefits of volunteering. He observed that "a loving and helpful life is more likely to be a happier, healthier, longer one." The meta-analysis showed that people who volunteer regularly experience lower levels of stress, aren't as likely to be depressed, and have a lower mortality rate. A few studies in "Good to Be Good" indicated that the people who exhibit these health benefits volunteer about two hours a week, which comes to a hundred hours a year.

Strong relationships are vital for a happy and healthy life. The strongest are those we actively seek and care for, that is, intentional efforts in service to others or to a larger community we are part of. As Annie Leonard, author of *The Story of Stuff*, points out, "When we act from our community or citizen selves, we can think more broadly. We consider the impact of our actions and we can broaden our thinking about strategies to make change." We do this by strengthening our social bonds, something social scientists refer to as social capital. A number of studies have shown that in times of distress, people survive and thrive by helping one another. That is why nurturing relationships and community is so important.

For example, a very small study followed five women volunteers over the course of three years. All of the women in the study had multiple sclerosis (MS), and they were chosen to act as "peer supporters for sixty-seven other MS patients." Volunteers were trained in active listening techniques and encouraged to call each patient once a month. Over the next three years the volunteers reported feelings of mastery, self-efficacy, and increased life satisfaction. This is great news because happiness spreads through social networks, which include neighbors, family members, and friends.

Most research shows you're likely to boost your happiness level by doing "hands-on" volunteer activities, but donating money to a cause you believe in will make you happy, too! It's what scholars call "pro-social spending." For instance, researchers at the University of British Columbia approached students and gave them a small amount of cash. Then the researchers randomly assigned students to spend the money on others or on themselves. At the end of the day, the students who spent the money on others were happier than those who spent the money on themselves.

Whether we give money or time, helping others has a powerful impact on social relationships. Personally, I've found that volunteering has given me a sense of belonging, new friendships, and a sense of purpose. It is perhaps the most direct way to create or join an intentional community.

Embrace Vulnerability, Exhibit Empathy

When I first moved to Portland, I was all by myself. Logan hadn't finished his PhD, so we lived apart for six months. Originally, Logan had planned on finishing his PhD in January 2010, but graduation was delayed until the summer. We only saw each other on the weekends, so I had to push myself to make new friends. This doesn't come naturally to me, and I was shy and nervous about it. Yet I knew that I couldn't rely on my charismatic husband to make connections for me. I had to get out into the community and meet people on my own.

Volunteering at Living Yoga was a start, but I wanted to do more. Then a blog reader sent me a link to the SHIFT website, which reads: "SHIFT revels in expressing Portland's creative bike culture through performance events and bike fun intended to highlight the positive contributions of bicycling for the community at large. As a loose-knit and informal bunch of bike-loving folks, we ask for no membership, nor dues, only a shared passion for the bicycle in all its glory: as toy, as transportation, as a tool for social and environmental change! SHIFT, then, is open to everyone sharing in this passion."

I couldn't resist this welcoming message. In California, Logan and I had evolved into avid cyclists, and lacking a car, we'd be joining the Portland biking community eventually. I decided to step out of my comfort zone and go for a bike ride. On the SHIFT calendar of events, Portland Pedal Tours was leading a Friday night Art by Bike Ride. As I sent out my RSVP email, my stomach felt like it dropped to the floor. The idea of going out by myself and talking to people I didn't know freaked me out a little!

When I showed up for the ride, I immediately met a dozen other people. The bike ride toured about five galleries in southwest Portland before finishing the night off with pizza and beer. It was a great experience, and as a result, I was invited out for several coffee dates and made several new friends. Stepping out of my comfort zone and making an active effort to engage with people were facilitated by my willingness to be vulnerable.

I keep coming back to these two words — *vulnerability* and *empathy*. They work together. Since I'm an avid cyclist, I strongly empathized with Portland's cycling community, and this helped me overcome my feelings of vulnerability. Conversely, being empathetic requires us to embrace our vulnerability. We should be concerned, and our concerns should lead us to act — helping and supporting others to create the world we want to see.

Face-to-face time is where true connections, friendships, and collaborative partnerships are created. For me community is about physical proximity, shared concerns, and real-life responsibilities. A community is there to help you get through rough patches. To highlight this point, here are a few stories sent to me by blog readers who are connected to their communities and are working on projects that will have a long-lasting impact.

> This summer I helped create a community garden in the Boyle Heights area of southern California. I am volunteering with a coalition of residents in my hometown of Montebello, California, to get bicycle lanes. I'm really proud of what I'm doing, and I feel that I have purpose!

> The church I attend has been running a food shelf for about three years now. It has turned into the largest food shelf in Minnesota. My husband and I volunteer. I think it has become such a success because of how we treat our guests. Yes, guests, not numbers. We give them a warm welcome, coffee, juice, and rolls while they wait, and a place to sit and relax. When we register them, we talk with them and offer to pray for any needs. I have often been in tears along with some of them as we pray for the difficulties in their lives. When their food is

> ready, someone takes it out and puts it in their car for them. We believe in serving our community with love and kindness. We have guests from not only the metro area but cities at least an hour away. We are open twice a week for only a couple hours but have an average of two hundred or more each time. They can only come once a month, so that adds up to at least a thousand different families served each month! It is humbling and a blessing to be able to be a part of this.
>
> I started a project to get my friends to cook for ourselves, together. It increases my connections, costs less than eating out (a common alternative for me), and builds a real resourcefulness within my friend circles.
>
> I find the greatest impact comes when the connection feels like it's one-on-one — even those made on a blog, twitter, or in a forum can feel quite personal and meaningful because ideas and insights are exchanged and a dialogue of understanding opens between two people. I volunteer in that same capacity — one-on-one mentorship. It's what helps me connect in a heartfelt way.

In Dr. Brené Brown's book *I Thought It Was Just Me*, she says, "What comes from the inside of us is a very human need to belong, to relate. We are hard wired for connection. It's in our biology. As infants, our need for connection is about survival. As we grow older, connection means thriving — emotionally, physically, spiritually, and intellectually." In short, we all have the need to be accepted, to belong, and to be appreciated for who we are. Community can help foster those things.

At its core, opening up and connecting with other people is what living simply is all about. It's about creating the intention to live mindfully and deliberately, and to constantly ask questions, not only about our living space, but also about our willingness to be vulnerable, be empathetic, and seek out community.

Micro-actions

- **Share and borrow stuff.** Rather than running out and buying the latest gadget, power tool, lawn mower, or hammer, consider borrowing the item. A variety of sharing cooperatives have popped up around the country. For example, there are tool libraries, bike-sharing programs, and even car shares like Zipcar. This isn't only about stuff. Offer to help your friends and family with child care, pet sitting, or taking care of their garden. Each time we share our time or resources, we avoid buying something new, and we make a meaningful connection with another human.
- **Volunteer.** I'd encourage you to check out www.volunteermatch.org. It's a website that will connect you to volunteer opportunities in your local community. Also, volunteer work doesn't have to be formal. For example, you could help friends plan a local event or even mentor work colleagues.
- **Introduce yourself to your neighbors.** The next time you feel lonely, knock on your neighbor's door. Drop by with a plate of cookies and invite them over for dinner sometime. We all have a community that literally surrounds us.
- **Go car-free or car-lite.** Ever since I went car-free, I'm more connected to my community. Initially, I thought selling my car would hinder my social life. But the opposite has occurred. I've connected to the local bike community, and I connect to fellow cyclists each time I ride.
- **Flex your "citizen muscle."** Flexing your citizen muscle will foster community connections on many levels. Are

there problems where you live that you'd like to see solved? Stand up and start solving them. Remember your community needs you as much as you need them. As Annie Leonard once noted in a book talk, "Reinvigorating your citizen muscle will rebuild public participation in politics and generate real collective solutions to the considerable problems we're facing on this planet."

CHAPTER 12

The Power of Tiny Pleasures

You have to participate relentlessly in the manifestations of your own blessings. And once you have achieved a state of happiness, you must never become lax about maintaining it. You must make a mighty effort to keep swimming upward into that happiness forever, to stay afloat on top of it.

— Elizabeth Gilbert

Chocolate ice cream was slowly dripping down my hand. The cone seemed to have sprung a leak, and no matter how fast I ate, I couldn't stop it. Chocolate was everywhere, and I was giggling. Not caring about the mess, I dragged Logan over to a flower stand on the corner. The flowers were so beautiful; I wanted one.

Logan shook his head in disbelief. "I'm surprised you're so interested in flowers. I used to buy them for you all the time, but you never seemed to like them. You told me they were a 'waste of money.'"

With sticky fingers, I picked up and admired a cabernet-colored peony. The women said I could have it for ninety-nine cents! In the past, I never bought cut flowers because it made me sad to see them wilt away. On that spring day, however, this particular flower made me strangely happy. I loved its shape, smell, and color. I decided to do something different and bought it.

When I got home, I put the peony in a small mason jar and added a little fresh cool water. I watched the flower open a little bit more every day, and to capture its beauty, I took a daily photo. Soon the peony resembled a simple corsage that someone would wear to a prom.

Humans are notoriously bad at predicting what will make them happy. We guess, ponder, and try to plot our lives. Indeed, I've spent plenty of time in my future dream world. Too often, I ignore the present moment and lose track of tiny pleasures. One major reason for simplifying my life the way I have has been to reverse this equation: to emphasize right now over what may or may not be tomorrow. We can't predict the future. We don't know what our lives will look like in ten years. But we can savor what we have right in front of us. We can engage our curiosity and make the most of our experiences.

Todd Kashdan noted in his book *Curious?*: "Given the near-universal desire to be happy, or at least happier than we are, we are surprisingly ignorant of what contributes to our happiness quotient." Kashdan's research shows that if you're constantly seeking out new information and experiences, and then integrating them into your life, new pathways form in your brain. This is great news, for it means it's possible to change bad habits and improve our well-being! For example, for no other reason than that he loved words and debating people, my grandpa Otto used to tilt back in his chair and flip through the pages of the dictionary, looking for new words to expand his language skills. Reading the dictionary, my grandpa let his curiosity loose, seeking to improve himself and explore new ideas and topics.

The day I bought my flower, I couldn't help thinking of Thornton Wilder's comment: "My advice to you is not to inquire why or whither, but just enjoy your ice cream while it's on your plate." There is a blissful perfection in even the smallest, most mundane facets of everyday life, and appreciating this is an important source of happiness. Happiness research has shown that people who savor life experiences are less neurotic and more self-confident. Interestingly, in a Belgian study, researchers discovered that the capacity to "savor" small pleasures was reduced among very wealthy individuals and that "constant access to any experience may undermine your happiness level." Humans adapt to any type of experience, but scholars suggest that we're less likely to adapt to tiny pleasures because, by their nature, they are unexpected and different each time they occur.

Happiness isn't a stroke of luck. It's something you have to practice every day. How? By choosing activities that spur your curiosity and engagement with the present moment. For example, I love practicing yoga; the blend of physicality and mindfulness works for me. Grandpa Otto read the dictionary. You might enjoy writing letters, reading books, going for long walks, or meeting and talking with friends. And occasionally, stopping to smell the flowers.

There is a lot of value to a simpler life — one that focuses on small acts of kindness, developing social connections, expressing gratitude, being mindful, and even purchasing a few tiny pleasures.

A Ripple of Kindness

During my midtwenties I was a volunteer coordinator at a rape crisis and domestic violence center in Northern California. Working with volunteers made me incredibly happy. They devoted hundreds of hours to the organization — answering crisis-line calls, accompanying victims to court, doing art projects with children at the shelter, raising money for the annual gala, and much, much more. Working with such a dynamic group of volunteers inspired me because they created a ripple effect of kindness within the agency and in the lives of the women, men, and children they helped.

Even though I was disheartened by the tragic stories I heard every day, I had the opportunity to watch women slowly rebuild their lives and rediscover joy and happiness. I witnessed what Dr. Sonja Lyubomirsky calls "constructing benefit in trauma," which she explains as "seeing some value in your loss or negative life event — for example, a change in perspective, a feeling that one's life has greater value, or a sense of personal growth." A lot of the women I worked with faced pain, sadness, and depression, but they focused on the positive events in their lives as well.

My experience in this field still provides me with constant reminders to be grateful for what I have — a loving family, friends, and an amazing life partner. And the thing is, I never would have had the privilege of working with survivors of domestic violence and sexual assault if I had stayed in the investment management industry. Working with victims of violence altered my perception of the world; it stretched me in a good way. I became cognizant of the importance of kindness and social support. Social support is critical to leading a happy and healthy life. A lot of the victims I worked with didn't have a close circle of friends or family members they could count on, and the agency fulfilled that role, providing basic resources for people in a time of need.

In addition, working at a domestic violence and rape crisis center taught me that you never know what kind of emotional baggage people are carrying around every day. Now, if I receive poor customer service or someone cuts me off in traffic, I do my best to be kind and nonjudgmental, rather than getting frustrated. Focusing on being kind and helpful is more than just a tiny pleasure; it adds a tremendous amount of joy and meaning to my life. Plus, being kind doesn't require any money. For me, an act of kindness is an expression of compassionate gratitude that increases my appreciation of what I already have.

I asked my blog readers about how they incorporate small acts of kindness in their everyday lives, and they shared a number of interesting stories.

> When I was young, my father told us a story about himself, to teach us to have compassion at an early age. When he was a young man, he was always impatient and hotheaded! Once he was in a movie theater with his date, and she wanted popcorn. They were sitting in the middle of the crowded theater. Everyone he passed in front of moved their legs so that he could maneuver more easily. At the end of the row was a young man who didn't move out of the way for my dad. My dad said out loud, "Well, don't trouble yourself to move, fella!" Then he proceeded to climb past him into the aisle. When the movie was over, the usher brought a wheelchair for the "fella" and had to lift him into it. You just never know. People who aren't smiling may be just barely holding back tears. I not only learned from this story but admired my father even more for telling it about himself.

> In the volunteer work I've done with kids, my favorite moments are when little kids run up and spontaneously hug me. It makes me feel so good knowing that I somehow impacted them at that moment. But what they don't know is that their sweet gesture made ME feel so much better, too!

> A while back I wrecked my car and it was not drivable. It was a Sunday, and the tow truck hauled my car to my house. The driver said I would have to get another tow truck on Monday to take it to a shop. As I was arguing with the driver, my neighbor walked into my garage and came out with my rotary mower. By the time I was finished with the driver, my lawn was almost completely mowed. I walked up to my neighbor to say thank you. I didn't even know his name. He said I looked

like I needed some kindness and insisted on finishing the lawn. I did need that kind act. We are good friends now.

A few years ago (during my time as a poor, struggling student) I couldn't afford to miss a day of work. I went in the very next day after a terrible, horrible, life-shattering event. I was there to make and serve people sandwiches, but spent the whole day simultaneously holding back tears and trying to remember how to breathe. A rude, pushy regular came in and started ordering me around, so I snapped back that I was busy and she'd need to wait her turn. She yelled at me, then complained to my supervisor. I wanted to die. I try to remember that, when I'm getting frustrated with someone, I have no idea what might be going on in their life, and I need to just give them a break. That lady made the most painful day of my life just a little bit worse, and I never want to do that to anyone!

Exercise and Happiness

Growing up, I could always be found on the ski slopes. In fact, my mom and dad met on a chairlift at a small ski resort called Homewood in Lake Tahoe, so perhaps it's only natural that I developed a love for downhill skiing and cold climates. My love for crisp air and the snow is part of my genetic coding.

I loved everything about skiing with my family. I loved drinking hot chocolate while I hung out with my dad in the ski patrol shack. I loved seeing Lake Tahoe glisten like a gem. More than anything, I loved skiing itself and how it was a shared family experience. Most of the time, my dad and I would race down the hill and wait for my mom to catch up.

After years spent skiing competitively and for fun, I stopped skiing regularly. The sport didn't feel fun to me anymore. In fact, during 2004, when I lived in Davis and worked at Franklin Templeton

Investments, I didn't even exercise regularly. That has taught me some powerful lessons about the relationship between exercise and happiness. When I neglect my body and don't exercise, I get cranky and tired, and my productivity falters. I'm unable to focus on creating good work or helping others. I knew this was true even while it was happening, but it was only when Logan and I got rid of our cars and I began biking every day that I truly appreciated it. When I move my body, the world is a happier, more interesting place.

In fact, researchers at Duke University found that a twenty-minute walk three times a week was more effective than being on an antidepressant. A similar result was described by the Gallup-Healthways Well-Being Index, which revealed, "Those who exercise at least two days per week report experiencing more happiness and less stress than those who do not." Perhaps this news isn't surprising, but it's worth remembering: physical exercise keeps you fit, gives you more energy, makes you feel less stressed, and even makes you more apt to be kind to others.

Naturally, exercising on your own is hard to maintain. I know I'm more apt to exercise if I can do it with a friend. Having a workout buddy motivates me to get out the door. For instance, when I lived in Davis, California, I swam every morning as part of a swim team. The program cost fifty dollars a month, but it meant I could swim every morning with friends and improve my techniques with the help of our coach. It wasn't always easy to jump into an outdoor pool (even one that was heated) at 6 AM, but I learned that by the end of practice I felt rejuvenated and ready to start my day. Similarly, a few years ago I was in a marathon-training program. I'd get up at 5 AM and meet my friend Kai for our scheduled early-morning run. Though I was self-motivated, I also knew I never would have trained without a running buddy. Knowing Kai would be waiting for me outside, I couldn't stay in bed.

So, if you want to increase your overall happiness, you need to exercise. And if you want to develop a good exercise routine, choose an activity you enjoy, that's cheap and easy to do regularly, and that you can do with others. If you don't enjoy the activity, you won't do it. You can run, bike, hike, or swim — but even a simple walk with a friend or your dog works, too. For myself, I also like to reward myself with a treat. For example, after my early-morning runs with Kai, we would stop for a large cup of coffee afterward. Somehow, I always appreciate coffee and treats more when I've done something to "earn" them, like running five to ten miles at the crack of dawn. It's well worth the investment in my well-being.

The Power of Gratitude and Memories

My grandmother Mabel's hands reminded me of twisted tree branches. She had arthritis throughout her body, but the disease seemed worst in her hands, where it acted like a vise that wouldn't let go. I think about my grandmother a lot. Waves of nostalgia sweep over me in unexpected moments, and before I know it I'm walking down memory lane. One moment that seems to be ingrained in my subconscious is the afternoon I heard about her death.

It was a sweltering summer day in Chico, and I had just dashed into my dorm room to cool off. It was 110 degrees that day, and I was grateful that the air-conditioning was still working. I immediately noticed that my old-school 1980s answering machine was beeping shrilly, like a smoke detector low on batteries. I had a phone message.

I hit the play button and heard my dad's voice, loud and clear, saying that my grandmother had passed away. My grandpa had died a few years earlier, and since that time my grandmother's health had continued to deteriorate. I knew this day would come, but it was still a shock.

I had so many questions I still wanted to ask her. How had my grandma felt on her first date? What was it like living through the

Great Depression? How did she feel growing up with eight siblings? Why were she and my great-aunt Mamie such good friends? Did her life turn out the way she expected?

Since her death, my dad has shared many family stories, but it's not the same as hearing my grandmother describe her own life. Yet even in the moment when I first dealt with the loss of my grandmother, I was overwhelmed with gratitude that she was part of my life for so long. As a little girl, I saw her often, and every time I reflect on the time we spent together, it makes me incredibly happy. Today, my memories are like the first bite of a warm cookie, when everything is perfect and sweet. I remember digging through a box of Lucky Charms as a five-year-old, picking out all the marshmallows and eating them, while Grandma watched *As the World Turns*. The sweet scent of hydrangeas wafted in through the front window. I felt safe and secure, like I was wrapped in a warm blanket.

I remember calling her after school using an old rotary phone that hung on the wall. It was an odd shade of yellow, and the receiver seemed bigger than my head. I loved talking to my grandma, and I love memories of that awkwardly large phone. As I've gotten older, I've realized that this is what life is made of — these small yet precious moments that go by in a flash.

Each time I remember my grandmother, I feel gratitude, which tempers my feelings of loss with appreciation and love for what we had. Studies show that regularly feeling and expressing gratitude makes us less stressed, depressed, and anxious (in particular, check out the book *Thanks!* by Robert Emmons). So, recently, I've been trying to develop a more self-conscious gratitude practice. Every day, I reflect on one or two things that I'm grateful for. In addition to performing these daily reflections, I've been collecting gratitude quotes. If I start feeling anxious or depressed, I reread these quotes. They help me realign my attitude and day. Here are a few:

Expressing gratitude is a natural state of being
and reminds us that we are all connected.

— Valerie Elster

The greatest part of our happiness depends
on our dispositions, not our circumstances.

— Martha Washington

Silent gratitude isn't much use to anyone.

— G. B. Stern

In ordinary life we hardly realize that we receive
a great deal more than we give,
and that it is only with gratitude that life becomes rich.

— Dietrich Bonhoeffer

My grandmother always told me, "You won't live forever, so practice gratitude every day." She had a knack for reminding me of what was really important when I was cranky or frustrated. I'm thankful for my grandmother's gentle reminder to integrate gratitude practices into my daily life. It is a reminder to be mindful in every moment.

A Walk in the Park

As I walked around the bend in the trail, a young man and woman were blocking my path. They were pointing up at the trees and gazing at the sky. It was a beautiful, sunny Sunday afternoon. The sky was a bright blue canvas lightly painted with broad white stripes.

I skirted around the pair and kept walking along the trail. The guy said, "Hey, Bear, where are you going?"

I turned around. Their black pit bull, Bear, was tugging on his leash and trying to follow me down the path.

I said, "Your dog is cute! He's ready for a run!"

"I know. Bear loves it out here. It's so beautiful."

As I turned to keep walking, the guy asked me, "Hey, do you know where we can find some free and fun stuff to do in Portland? We just moved up here from California."

"Really? Where in California?"

"We're from Shasta County."

"No way!" I exclaimed. "I'm from Red Bluff."

"Cool! It's nice to meet you!"

He stretched out his hand. We shook and made official introductions: he was Brian; his girlfriend was Lucy; and then there was Bear, their pit bull, and their tiny cat, Scarlet. Scarlet was hiding in Lucy's purse. The kitten was probably two months old and had a tiny white bandanna around her neck. Scarlet jumped out of Lucy's purse and ran down the trail. I was worried at first, until I saw she had on a leash. Scarlet rolled around in the dirt, where a sunbeam had peeked through the trees. She stood up, shook off a layer of dirt, and looked very proud of herself.

As I told Brian about free stuff to do in Portland, he said, "We moved up here to escape the gangs and meth problems in Redding. Plus, we're taking care of my grandpa. He lives in Vancouver, and we're trying to figure out where to live."

Brian asked me a lot of other questions about housing and transportation, and I did my best to be helpful. Eventually, I wished them the best of luck and took off down the trail.

My conversation with this young couple stayed with me all the way back to our tiny house. They reminded me of Logan and myself and of how far we've come. The couple seemed so young to be dealing with so many major life challenges. It made me grateful for my own good fortune. My concerns always seem so trite when compared to the problems that so many people, like this young couple, must overcome.

I do my best to operate from a place of kindness, rather than judgment. I'm not perfect and judgment still creeps into my consciousness. But the trick is being aware of that tendency, rather than blocking it out. This brief conversation reminded me of my old life: driving everywhere, going to a job I hated, and not spending enough time outside. I was so "busy" then, I probably wouldn't have slowed down long enough to chat with the couple in the park.

In fact, I probably wouldn't even have been in the park. In this way, at least, the young couple didn't need my help: they already knew that, no matter where you live, the woods and parks, the trees, sky, and sun are free and only waiting to be enjoyed. You never know what you'll learn from a walk in the park.

You Can't Ignore Nature

As my friend Dee recently said, "You can't ignore nature when you're living in such a small space."

As I write these words, the sun is setting just over Portland's western hills. The colors — pink, purple, and orange — seem too bright and rich to be real. I'm snuggled up under my fleece blanket, in my tiny loft, waiting for Logan to get home from the office. Our cat, Elaina, is crying. She wants to go outside and explore. I can't blame her. I'm sure the wet grass feels good on her soft, pink paws. Yesterday, she dug a hole in the dirt for the first time. It was the cutest thing I've seen all week. Even though she's cute, I'm not giving in. She's allowed outside during the day, but not at night because there are coyotes who like to hang out on the bluff.

We learned this a few weeks ago, when we heard our neighbor shouting for one of her dogs, Nola. Logan and I put our shoes on, walked briskly over to the side yard, and asked if everything was okay. Karen said, "We're fine. Sorry to scare you guys. I thought Nola was being eaten by coyotes!"

As we wandered back to our little house, Logan shined his bike lamp down the hill. The bright orbs of coyote eyes reflected back at us. The thought of scavengers and other creatures staring at us in the dark totally freaked me out. That's why I'm okay with listening to Elaina cry in the evenings. I don't want her to become a midnight snack.

Elaina finally stopped crying and climbed up the loft ladder. She plopped down next to me and looked at my journal, as if to encourage me to keep writing. Then she proceeded to flop down on the blanket and lick her big, fat belly. She looks like Jabba the Hut, but I'm hoping that will change with her new routine. Running around outside during the day is giving her a serious workout. In fact, living this close to nature is going to keep us all in shape, though it isn't without its own challenges, like nocturnal coyotes.

I'm constantly amazed at how my life is unfolding. My life looks completely different than I thought it would ten years ago, and I'm extremely happy. I have a beautiful home, one more in tune with the rhythms of nature.

Micro-actions

This chapter only covers the tip of the iceberg. Ultimately, tiny pleasures, curiosity, and mindfulness are what provide us with the big things we desire: kindness, social support, satisfaction, gratitude, and happiness. How can you cultivate more tiny pleasures in your own life?

- **Make a list of your current tiny pleasures.** What little things bring you joy and happiness? How often do you do them? How can you incorporate more of them into your own life? Planning for tiny pleasures is one way to ensure you focus on them and appreciate them. Even better: How many unexpected, unlooked-for tiny pleasures can you list at the end of each day?

- **Do something kind for another person every day.** In essence, our kind actions create a ripple of kindness in our lives and in the lives of others. An act of kindness doesn't have to be large, and it can involve a friend or a stranger. Merely setting the intention to be kind is sometimes all the inspiration we need. Consider donating blood, writing a thank-you letter, or taking a friend out for dinner.
- **Ruminate less.** I tend to be a worrywart, and it's something I'm trying to change. It's not easy, and it requires practice, but it's worth it. I'm happier when I'm not worrying about writing or what other people think of me. If you're dealing with a problem that's causing you to worry, take action to solve that problem. Identify one or two small steps you can take today. Maybe this means making a phone call, contacting a therapist, or writing down a list of solutions that can solve the problem.
- **Identify one thing you can do every day to improve a skill.** I love photography and I'm trying to enhance my picture-taking abilities. During 2012, I committed to taking one photo a day and posting that photo to my blog or Google+. So far the exercise has been challenging, and it's brought me a lot of happiness too, because my photos continue to get better!

EPILOGUE

Love Life, Not Stuff

Learning to live simply has brought an incredible amount of joy to my life. But it's an ongoing process, and I'm still learning. I'm dedicated to loving life, not stuff (to quote Leo Babauta), yet sometimes that isn't as simple as it seems. As I close this book, I want to share a final story.

After celebrating the 2011 Thanksgiving holiday with Logan's parents in Yreka, California, Logan and I returned home in our Zipcar. It was a long highway drive through the rain, and by the time we got out of the car, I felt stiff and uncomfortable. My whole body felt angry with me, and needless to say, I was happy to stretch my legs. After returning our Zipcar, we had a mile-and-a-half walk to our little house.

As Logan and I walked home, we started talking about our bills.

Soon, I felt a familiar financial anxiety creep up my spine, along with a different, even more troubling unease.

To buy our little house, Logan and I spent all of our savings and took a small, interest-free, five-thousand-dollar loan from my parents. Both my mom and dad said they would be happy to help us make our dream a reality, and they were adamant that they wouldn't charge interest on the loan. We were grateful and agreed. But even though we had a plan for becoming debt-free again by spring of 2012, and I already knew how I would thank my parents once we were, I didn't feel better.

I looked out over Swan Island, an industrial hub in Portland, whose lights looked like bright stars sitting on a layer of fog and told Logan, "Being in debt again, I feel like a failure. I feel like I've let myself and my readers down. I feel like an impostor."

Logan dodged a puddle and asked, "Tammy, why do you feel like an impostor?"

"I'm an advocate of being debt-free, and here I am in debt again. It feels like a huge setback. I do my best to live by my values, but with our tiny house I sacrificed money for a long-term investment. I don't think that's a bad thing, but I'm scared that people will judge me."

Logan did his best to reassure me. When I worry, I often lose perspective. As for the money, he encouraged me to "look at the five-thousand-dollar loan as an investment, not a burden. Don't let anxiety take over. Remember to breathe and listen to your own advice."

"You're right," I said. "We have more than enough and that makes me happy and grateful. Sometimes I feel like I have to learn the same lessons over and over again."

The things in life that are worth doing aren't easy. Getting rid of stuff, avoiding debt, and making big career changes aren't easy. It's ironic that pursuing simplicity can be so complex; in our effort to create a debt-free lifestyle, Logan and I had to go into debt again, at least briefly. I didn't like it, but these are the sorts of compromises and challenging situations that, in the long run, we all have to negotiate to build happier lives. I hadn't abandoned my core principles to build our tiny house; instead, I had to let go of my idealized vision of what my quest for a simple, happy, and authentic life should look like. In *The Gifts of Imperfection*, Dr. Brené Brown defines authenticity as "the daily practice of letting go of who we think we're supposed to be and embracing who we are."

To live a truly happy, joyous life I've learned that I have to be my own authentic, imperfect self. When I get stuck and frustrated, I remember what my friend Chris O'Byrne says about happiness, that "there is no way to happiness; happiness is the way." Life is not going to conform to our ideals, but we can still appreciate what we are able to achieve, we can accept life with gratitude, and we can find joy daily in tiny pleasures.

Building our little house was an opportunity we couldn't pass up. By taking on a little debt, our life became more complicated. But in the long run, living in the little house will enable us to focus on our relationships, our community, and giving back. Once I've paid my parents back, I plan on starting a separate savings account, and I will use that money to help friends and family members the way my parents helped us.

Every day, living in such a tiny dwelling is a constant reminder to love life, not stuff. The house symbolizes my guiding principles. Another symbol in my life is my hydrangea tattoo, which runs the full length of my upper left arm. Each blossom represents a person in my family. Specifically, Great-Aunt Mamie, Grandpa Otto, and Grandma Mabel. Every time I look in the mirror I'm reminded of the lessons they taught me about happiness. I remember my grandpa's love of the dictionary, watching soap operas with my grandma, and playing with the toys in the tiny red box my aunt Mamie set aside for me.

Looking back, I find it hard to believe that the same kid who once savored small pleasures became such a materialistic young adult. Ten years ago, I felt like I "deserved" nice things in my life, like a big diamond ring, a new car, and an ever-greater living space. After acquiring these things, I realized life is too valuable to be spent chasing possessions. Trading my time for the money to buy a "cool" identity, a car, and a big house seems like no kind of bargain at all.

Conversely, for me, living simply isn't about becoming an ascetic; it's not about denying yourself pleasure and joy. It's not about austerity. Instead, it's about building a life steeped in the only precious gifts that can bring lasting happiness: time, freedom, and community. The focus is on life, not stuff. It's my hope that this book will help you to cultivate strong relationships and intentional communities and to appreciate the constant pleasures of a life lived simply.

Endnotes

During late 2010 and throughout 2011, I interviewed dozens of people for this book; I conducted interviews either in person or on the telephone. However, some people have chosen not to identify themselves; to protect their privacy, I've changed certain names, along with identifying information. Some people I interviewed have their own blogs and websites; see Resources & Further Reading for a list.

Introduction: Rethinking Normal

Page 1, *It all started with a short YouTube video featuring Dee Williams:* Dee Williams, "Dream House: Featuring Dee Williams" NAU, November 6, 2006, http://www.youtube.com/watch?v=eZM2G-PfEbc.

Page 1, *In one article, she described a trip she took to Guatemala:* Carol Estes, "Living Large in a Tiny House," *Yes!*, October 31, 2008, http://www.yesmagazine.org/issues/sustainable-happiness/living-large-in-a-tiny-house.

Page 2, *Dee's story inspired me to go small and start thinking big:* For more, see Stephen Post, "It's Good to Be Good: 2011 Fifth Annual Scientific Report on Health, Happiness, and Helping Others," the Institute for Research on Unlimited Love, Case Western Reserve University, 2011, http://www.unlimitedloveinstitute.org/publications/pdf/Good_to_be_Good_2011.pdf; and Stephen Post, "Altruism, Happiness, and Health: It's Good to Be Good," *International Journal of Behavioral Medicine* 12, no. 5 (2005): 66-77.

Page 2, *For instance, in September 2011 the nation's poverty rate:* Details from Pam Fessler, "Census: 2011 Saw Poverty Rate Increase, Income Drop," NPR, September 23, 2011, http://www.npr.org/2011/09/13/140438725/census-2010-saw-poverty-rate-increase-income-drop; and Mellody Hobson, "Mellody's Math: Credit Card Cleanup," *ABC News*, February 28, 2009, http://abcnews.go.com/GMA/FinancialSecurity/story?id=126244&page=1.

Chapter 1: Buying Things Will Not Make You Happy

Page 10, *According to the Happy Planet Index, conducted by the New Economics Foundation:* "The Happy Planet Index 2.0: Why Good Lives Don't Have to Cost the Earth," New Economics Foundation, 2009, http://www.happyplanetindex.org/learn/download-report.html.

Page 11, *For instance, in 1976, researchers surveyed:* J. H. Pryor and others, "The American Freshman — National Norms for Fall 2005," Higher Education Research Institute, University of California at Los Angeles, 2006.

Page 11, *Samuel Alexander and Simon Ussher, researchers at a think tank called the Simplicity Institute:* Samuel Alexander and Simon Ussher, "The Voluntary Simplicity Movement: A Multi-national Survey

Analysis in Theoretical Context," Simplicity Institute, http://simplicityinstitute.org/publications.

Chapter 2: The Stuff You Own Owns You

Page 19, *Before I simplified my life, I was buying so much stuff:* Details in this paragraph are from Facts & Trends Reports, Self Storage Association, http://www.selfstorage.org/; and Michelle Hofmann, "The S-t-r-e-t-c-h Garage," *Los Angeles Times*, October 1, 2006, http://articles.latimes.com/2006/oct/01/realestate/re-garages1.

Page 20, *Every year on Black Friday millions of Americans:* Details in this paragraph are from "Black Friday," *New York Times*, November 28, 2011, http://topics.nytimes.com/top/reference/timestopics/subjects/r/retail_stores_and_trade/black_friday/index.html; and Stephanie Clifford, "Shoppers Flock to the Mall to Hunt Deals," *New York Times*, November 26, 2010, http://www.nytimes.com/2010/11/27/business/27shop.html?_r=1.

Page 20, *Do you remember Jdimytai Damour, a Walmart worker:* Ken Belson and Karen Zraick, "Mourning a Good Friend, and Trying to Make Sense of a Stampede," *New York Times*, November 29, 2008, http://www.nytimes.com/2008/11/30/nyregion/30walmart.html.

Page 21, *In 2010, a Target shopper in Buffalo, New York:* Rich Newberg, "Shopper Rushed to Hospital after Trampling," WIVB, November 26, 2010, http://www.wivb.com/dpp/news/buffalo/Shopper-rushed-to-hospital-after-trampling.

Page 22, *Study after study has shown that debt can have a negative impact:* R. Jenkins and others, "Debt, Income and Mental Disorder in the General Population," *Psychological Medicine* 38 (2008): 1485–93.

Page 22, *In July 2008, a fifty-three-year-old Massachusetts woman named Carlene Balderrama:* Michael Levenson, "The Anguish of Foreclosure," *Boston Globe*, July 24, 2008, http://www.boston.com/news/local/articles/2008/07/24/the_anguish_of_foreclosure/.

Page 22, *That same month a sixty-two-year-old New Jersey man named Emilio Saladriagas:* Kasi Addison, "Newark Man Sets Himself on

Fire," NJ.com, July 30, 2008, http://www.nj.com/news/index.ssf/2008/07/newark_man_sets_himself_on_fire.html.

Page 25, *For example,* USA Today *reported that the average undergraduate:* Kathy Chu, "Average College Credit Card Debt Rises with Fees, Tuition," *USA Today*, April 13, 2009, http://www.usatoday.com/money/perfi/credit/2009-04-12-college-credit-card-debt_N.htm.

Page 27, *Research suggests that people care more deeply about what others think:* T. Kasser and K. M. Sheldon, "Of Wealth and Death: Materialism, Mortality Salience, and Consumption Behavior," *Psychological Science* 11 (2000): 348–51.

Page 27, *Frank and other scholars argue that people spend money:* S. Lyubomirsky and L. Ross, "Hedonic Consequences of Social Comparison: A Contrast of Happy and Unhappy People," *Journal of Personality and Social Psychology* 73 (1997): 1141–57.

Chapter 4: The Power of Debt

Page 49, *According to researchers, writing down goals can help:* L. A. King, "The Health Benefits of Writing about Life Goals," *Personality and Social Psychology Bulletin* 27 (2001): 798–807.

Page 49, *The auto club AAA estimates that the average American spends:* Behind the Numbers: Your Driving Costs, AAA, 2009, http://www.aaaexchange.com/Assets/Files/200948913570.DrivingCosts2009.pdf.

Page 50, *Studies back up my experience. Getting enough exercise:* Elizabeth Mendes, "In U.S., Nearly Half Exercise Less Than Three Days a Week," *Gallup*, May 26, 2009, http://www.gallup.com/poll/118570/nearly-half-exercise-less-three-days-week.aspx; and S. J. H. Biddle and P. Ekkekakis, "Physically Active Lifestyles and Wellbeing," in *The Science of Well-being* (New York: Oxford University Press, 2006), 141–64.

Page 51, *In addition to the services Gansky mentioned, Hertz is introducing:* Mark Vanhoenacker, "Hertz on Demand Enters Car-Sharing Race," *New York Times*, September 8, 2011, http://intransit.blogs.nytimes.com/2011/09/08/hertz-on-demand-enters-car-sharing-race/.

Page 53, *According to a 2011 article in* The Atlantic *magazine:* Richard Florida, "The Financial Benefits of Living in Transit-Friendly, Walkable Areas," *The Atlantic*, June 8, 2011, http://www.theatlantic.com/business/archive/2011/06/the-financial-benefits-of-living-in-transit-friendly-walkable-areas/240075/; also, Wendy Koch, "Study: Walkable Neighborhoods Have Happier People," *USA Today*, December 10, 2010, http://content.usatoday.com/communities/greenhouse/post/2010/12/walkable-neighborhoods-happy-people/1.

Chapter 5: Sell What You Can, Give the Rest Away

Page 66, *I frequently remember a powerful talk my friend Dee Williams once gave:* Dee Williams, "Dream Big, Live Small," TEDxConcordiaU-Portland, 2011, http://tedxtalks.ted.com/video/TEDxConcordiaUPortland-Dee-Will.

Page 69, *A 1978 study by psychologist Philip Brickman:* Philip Brickman, "Lottery Winners and Accident Victims: Is Happiness Relative?" *Journal of Personality and Social Psychology* 36 (1978): 917.

Page 77, *Interestingly, researchers from Yale University and the University of New Hampshire:* M. Clark and others, "Heightened Interpersonal Security Diminishes the Monetary Value of Possessions," *Journal of Experimental Social Psychology* 47 (2010): 359–64.

Chapter 7: Reclaiming Work

Page 108, *The story ended up running on the front page of the* New York Times' *Sunday business section:* The newspaper story in which I was featured was Stephanie Rosenbloom, "But Will It Make You Happy?" *New York Times*, August 7, 2010, http://www.nytimes.com/2010/08/08/business/08consume.html?_r=4&pagewanted=1. See also, "Can Money Buy Happiness?" *The Today Show*, 2010, http://today.msnbc.msn.com/id/26184891/vp/38655998%2338655998#38655998.

Chapter 8: Time Is the Only Real Wealth

Page 118, *For instance, in 2007, Princeton economist Alan Krueger published a fascinating paper:* Alan B. Krueger, "Are We Having More Fun Yet? Categorizing and Evaluating Changes in Time Allocation," *Project Muse*, 2008, http://muse.jhu.edu/journals/eca/summary/v2007/2007.2krueger.html.

Page 118, *Interestingly, one study examined how focusing on personal time:* C. Mogilner, "The Pursuit of Happiness: Time, Money, and Social Connection," *Psychological Science* 21, no. 9 (2010): 1348–54.

Page 119, *In a study called "Stress That Doesn't Pay: The Commuting Paradox":* Alois Stutzer and Bruno Frey, "Stress That Doesn't Pay: The Commuting Paradox" (working paper, Institute for Empirical Research in Economics, University of Zurich, 2004), http://econpapers.repec.org/paper/zuriewwpx/151.htm.

Page 122, *Today, the average American home contains more TVs than people:* For details in this paragraph, see Bureau of Labor Statistics, "American Time Use Survey," http://www.bls.gov/tus/ (accessed 2009); and Alana Semuels, "Television Viewing at All-Time High," *Los Angeles Times*, February 24, 2009, http://articles.latimes.com/2009/feb/24/business/fi-tvwatching24.

Page 124, *In September 2010, the Chartered Institute for IT released an intriguing report:* "The Information Dividend: Why IT Makes You 'Happier,'" the Chartered Institute for IT, September 2010, http://www.bcs.org/content/conWebDoc/35476.

Page 125, *A number of researchers and reporters have found that constantly scrolling through email:* The relationship between technology and happiness is a hot topic. Here are several articles I referenced while writing this book: Matt Richtel, "Attached to Technology and Paying a Price," *New York Times*, June 6, 2010, http://www.nytimes.com/2010/06/07/technology/07brain.html?pagewanted=1&ref=matt_richtel; Matt Richtel, "Growing Up Digital, Wired for Distraction," *New York Times*, November 21, 2010, http://www.nytimes.com/2010/11/21/technology/21brain.html?ref=yourbrainoncomputers; Matt Richtel, interview by Terri Gross, "Digital Overload: Your Brain on Gadgets," National Public Radio, August 24,

2010, http://www.npr.org/templates/story/story.php?storyId=129384107; and Libby Copeland, "The Anti-social Network: By Helping Other People Look Happy, Facebook Is Making Us Sad," *Slate*, January 26, 2011, http://www.slate.com/id/2282620/. Also see the books *Alone Together* by Sherry Turkle and *Hamlet's BlackBerry* by William Powers.

Page 125, *Sherry Turkle has written extensively about people's relationship with technology:* Sherry Turkle, interview by Krista Tippett, "Alive Enough?" the Civil Conversation Project, On Being series, American Public Radio, September 1, 2011, http://being.publicradio.org/programs/2011/ccp-turkle/.

Page 125, *Journalist Marjorie Connelly reported in the* New York Times*:* Marjorie Connelly, "More Americans Sense a Downside to an Always Plugged-In Existence," *New York Times*, June 6, 2010, http://www.nytimes.com/2010/06/07/technology/07brainpoll.html?ref=technology.

Chapter 9: Money vs. Experiences

Page 132, *As Scott Russell Sanders noted in an article entitled "Breaking the Spell of Money":* Scott Russell Sanders, "Breaking the Spell of Money," *Orion*, July/August 2011, http://www.orionmagazine.org/index.php/articles/article/6343/.

Page 135, *In recent papers, Dunn and her colleagues explained that income:* Elizabeth W. Dunn, D. Gilbert, and T. Wilson, "If Money Doesn't Make You Happy Then You Probably Aren't Spending It Right," *Journal of Consumer Psychology* (2010); L. Aknin, M. I. Norton, and Elizabeth W. Dunn, "From Wealth to Well-Being? Money Matters, but Less Than People Think," *Journal of Positive Psychology* 4 (2009): 523–27.

Chapter 10: Relationships Matter, Not Things

Page 142, *Relationships can't be overlooked, because they surround us every moment:* Here is some of the happiness research I found:

R. F. Baumeister and others, "Social Rejection Can Reduce Pain and Increase Spending: Further Evidence That Money, Pain, and Belongingness Are Interrelated," *Psychological Inquiry* 19 (2008): 145–47; E. Berscheid, "The Human's Greatest Strength: Other Humans," in *A Psychology of Human Strengths: Fundamental Questions and Future Directions for a Positive Psychology*, ed. L. G. Aspinwall and U. M. Staudinger (Washington, DC: American Psychological Association, 2003); and D. Buettner, "New Wrinkles on Aging," *National Geographic*, November 2005.

Chapter 11: The Art of Community Building

Page 158, *Stephen Post is the director of the Institute for Research on Unlimited Love:* Stephen Post, "It's Good to be Good: 2011 Fifth Annual Scientific Report on Health, Happiness, and Helping Others," the Institute for Research on Unlimited Love, Case Western Reserve University, 2011, http://www.unlimitedloveinstitute.org/publications/pdf/Good_to_be_Good_2011.pdf;

Page 159, *A number of studies have shown that in times of distress:* For instance, one study showing the benefits of nurturing relationships is M. Y. Barlett and D. DeSteno, "Gratitude and Prosocial Behavior: Helping When It Costs You," *Psychological Science* 17 (2006): 319–25. For a general review of the benefits of volunteering, see the material produced by the Corporation for National and Community Service, www.nationalservice.gov. See also *Volunteering in America* (2009), produced by the US government; http://www.volunteeringinamerica.gov.

Page 159, *For example, a very small study followed five women volunteers:* C. E. Schwartz and M. Sendor, "Helping Others Helps Oneself: Response Shift Effects in Peer Support," *Social Science and Medicine* 48 (1999): 1563–75.

Page 160, *Then a blog reader sent me a link to the SHIFT website, which reads:* Quote is from the Shift 2 Bikes "Who We Are" website page, http://shift2bikes.org/whoWeAre.php.

Chapter 12: The Power of Tiny Pleasures

Page 167, *Interestingly, in a Belgian study, researchers discovered that the capacity:* The Belgian study is described in F. B. Bryant and J. Veroff, *Savoring: A New Model of Positive Experience* (Mahwah, NJ: Erlbaum, 2006).

Page 168, *I witnessed what Dr. Sonja Lyubomirsky calls "constructing benefit in trauma":* Dr. Lyubomirsky is quoted in R. G. Tedeschi and L. G. Calhoun, "Posttraumatic Growth: Conceptual Foundations and Empirical Evidence," *Psychological Inquiry* 15 (2004): 1–18.

Page 171, *Perhaps this news isn't surprising, but it's worth remembering:* physical exercise keeps you fit: G. B. Sullivan and M. J. Sullivan, "Promoting Wellness in Cardiac Rehabilitation: Exploring the Role of Altruism," *Journal of Cardiovascular Nursing*, 11, no. 3 (1997): 43–52.

Page 173, *every time I reflect on the time we spent together, it makes me incredibly happy:* For a more scientific look at the benefits of happy memories, see F. B. Bryant, C. M. Smart, and S. P. King, "Using the Past to Enhance the Present: Boosting Happiness through Positive Reminiscence," *Journal of Happiness Studies* 6 (2005): 227–60.

Page 173, *Each time I remember my grandmother, I feel gratitude:* For more on the positive effects of gratitude, see B. L. Fredrickson and others, "What Good Are Positive Emotions in Crises?: A Prospective Study of Resilience and Emotions Following the Terrorist Attacks on the United States in September 11, 2001," *Journal of Personality and Social Psychology* 84 (2003): 365–76; and P. C. Watkins, D. L. Grimm, and R. Kolts, "Counting Your Blessings: Positive Memories Amount to Grateful Persons," *Current Psychology: Developmental, Learning, Personality, Social* 23 (2004): 52–67.

Page 177, *This chapter only covers the tip of the iceberg:* For more on the benefits of mindfulness, see K. W. Brown, and R. M. Ryan, "The Benefits of Being Present: Mindfulness and Its Role in Psychological Well-Being," *Journal of Personality and Social Psychology* 84 (2003): 822–48.

Resources and Further Reading

Books

Bok, Derek. *The Politics of Happiness: What Government Can Learn from the New Research on Well-Being*. Princeton, NJ: Princeton University Press, 2010.

Brown, Brené. *The Gifts of Imperfection: Let Go of Who You Think You're Supposed to Be and Embrace Who You Are*. Minnesota: Hazelden, 2010.

———. *I Thought It Was Just Me (but It Isn't): Telling the Truth about Perfectionism, Inadequacy, and Power*. New York: Gotham Books, 2007.

Bruno, Dave. *The 100 Thing Challenge: How I Got Rid of Almost Everything, Remade My Life, and Regained My Soul*. New York: Harper, 2010.

Claiborne, Shane. *The Irresistible Revolution: Living as an Ordinary Radical*. Grand Rapids, MI: Zondervan, 2006.

De Graaf, John, David Wann, and Thomas H. Naylor. *Affluenza: The All-Consuming Epidemic*. 2nd ed. San Fransciso: Berrett-Koehler Publishers, 2005.

Emmons, Robert A. *Thanks!: How the New Science of Gratitude Can Make You Happier*. New York: Houghton Mifflin Harcourt, 2007.

Frank, Robert. *Luxury Fever: Weighing the Cost of Excess*. Princeton, NJ: Princeton University Press, 2010.

Frost, Randy, and Gail Steketee. *Stuff: Compulsive Hoarding and the Meaning of Things*. New York: Houghton Mifflin Harcourt, 2010.

Gansky, Lisa. *The Mesh: Why the Future of Business Is Sharing*. New York: Portfolio, 2010.

Gottman, John, and Nan Silver. *The Seven Principles for Making Marriage Work*. New York: Portfolia, 1999.

Guillebeau, Chris. *The Art of Non-conformity: Set Your Own Rules, Live the Life You Want, and Change the World*. New York: Perigee Trade, 2010.

Hanson, Rick, and Richard Mendius. *Buddha's Brain: The Practical Neuroscience of Happiness, Love, and Wisdom*. Oakland, CA: New Harbinger Publications, 2009.

Heinberg, Richard. *The End of Growth: Adapting to Our New Economic Reality*. Gabriola Island, BC: New Society Publishers, 2011.

Kashdan, Todd. *Curious?: Discover the Missing Ingredient to a Fulfilling Life*. New York: William Morrow, 2009.

Kasser, Tim. *The High Price of Materialism*. Boston: Bradford Books, 2002.

Kilbourne, Jean. *Can't Buy My Love: How Advertising Changes the Way We Think and Feel*. New York: Free Press, 2000.

Layard, Richard. *Happiness: Lessons from a New Science*. New York: Penguin Press, 2004.

Lehrer, Jonah. *How We Decide*. New York: Houghton Mifflin, 2009.

Leleux, Robert. *The Living End: A Memoir of Forgetting and Forgiving*. New York: St. Martin's Press, 2012.

Leonard, Annie. *The Story of Stuff: How Our Obsession with Stuff Is*

Trashing the Planet, Our Communities, and Our Health — And a Vision for Change. New York: The Free Press, 2010.

Levine, Madeline. *The Price of Privilege: How Parental Pressure and Material Advantage Are Creating a Generation of Disconnected and Unhappy Kids*. New York: Harper Collins, 2006.

Lovenheim, Peter. *In the Neighborhood: The Search for Community on an American Street, One Sleepover at a Time*. New York: Perigee Trade, 2010.

Lyubomirsky, Sonja. *The How of Happiness: A New Approach to Getting the Life You Want*. New York: Penguin, 2008.

Marcos, Subcomandante Insurgente. *Our Word Is Our Weapon: Selected Writings*. Edited by Juana Ponce de León. New York: Seven Stories Press, 2002.

Martin, Paul. *One Man's Leg: A Memoir*. Pine Bush, NY: GreyCore Press, 2002.

McKibben, Bill. *Deep Economy: The Wealth of Communities and the Durable Future*. New York: Henry Holt, 2007.

Nolen-Hoeksema, Susan. *Eating, Drinking, Overthinking: The Toxic Triangle of Food, Alcohol, and Depression — and How Women Can Break Free*. New York: Henry Holt, 2005.

Post, Stephen G. *The Hidden Gifts of Helping: How the Power of Giving, Compassion, and Hope Can Get Us through Hard Times*. San Francisco: Jossey-Bass, 2011.

Powers, William. *Hamlet's BlackBerry: A Practical Philosophy for Building a Good Life in the Digital Age*. New York: Harper, 2010.

Putnam, Robert. *Bowling Alone: The Collapse and Revival of American Community*. New York: Simon & Schuster, 2001.

Rinpoche, Yongey Mingyur, and Eric Swanson. *The Joy of Living: Unlocking the Secret and Science of Happiness*. New York: Harmony, 2007.

Robin, Vicki, Joe Dominguez, and Monique Tilford. *Your Money or Your Life: 9 Steps to Transforming Your Relationship with Money and Achieving Financial Independence*. Rev. ed. New York: Penguin, 2008.

Rubin, Gretchen. *The Happiness Project: Or, Why I Spent a Year Trying to Sing in the Morning, Clean My Closets, Fight Right, Read Aristotle, and Generally Have More Fun*. New York: Harper, 2009.

Salomon, Shay. *Little House on a Small Planet: Simple Homes, Cozy Retreats, and Energy Efficient Possibilities*. Connecticut: Lyons Press, 2006.

Schor, Juliet. *The Overworked American: The Unexpected Decline of Leisure*. New York: Basic Books, 1991.

Taylor, Jill Bolte. *My Stroke of Insight: A Brain Scientist's Personal Journey*. New York: Viking Adult, 2008.

Turkle, Sherry. *Alone Together: Why We Expect More from Technology and Less from Each Other*. New York: Basic Books, 2011.

Twitchell, James B. *Branded Nation*. New York: Simon & Schuster, 2004.

Vanderkam, Laura. *168 Hours: You Have More Time Than You Think*. New York: Penguin, 2010.

Worldwatch Institute. *State of the World 2004: Special Focus — Consumer Society*. New York: W.W. Norton & Company, 2004.

Websites & Blogs

There are hundreds of websites and blogs dedicated to living simply, tiny homes, and happiness. Below are a few of my favorite resources. They have helped me on my journey, and I hope these sites will help you, too!

Simple Living and Happiness

- **www.becomingminimalist.com** by Joshua Becker is about "a rational approach to minimalism."
- **www.bemorewithless.com** by Courtney Carver is "a blog about simplifying your life and really living."
- Lindsey Hoffman is visiting a series of intentional communities across the United States; follow her journey at **Foreverarriving.blogspot.com.**

- **www.getrichslowly.org/blog** by J. D. Roth is a wonderful resource if you need help with your finances.
- Gwen Bell writes about a variety of topics, like business, travel, experience telling, and yoga, as well as attention and awareness training. Learn more at **www.gwenbell.com.**
- **www.happyplanetindex.org** has a wealth of data, reports, and news about happiness research, consumerism, and living sustainably.
- **www.happiness-project.com** by Gretchen Rubin is all about happiness, all the time. It's one of many sites that inspired me to start writing more often.
- **jolieguillebeau.com.** I have only one piece of art in my home and it's by Jolie Guillebeau. You can learn more about her beautiful paintings at her website.
- Francine Jay believes that "minimalism isn't about emptiness for the sake of emptiness — but rather making room to move freely, think clearly, and open ourselves to the beauty and wonder of life." Read more at **www.missminimalist.com.**
- Russ Roca and Laura Crawford sold all their belongings in 2009 and have been traveling the country by bicycle ever since: **PathLessPedaled.com.**
- **simplicityinstitute.org** is a think tank that studies "post-consumerist lifestyles," via qualitative and quantitative research.
- **SmashedPicketFences.com** by Tina Smith hosts her nonfiction writing, very humorous stories about being a parent, recipes, and more.
- **Thestonesoup.com/blog** is full of simple, easy, and healthy recipes.
- If you're ready to change your career or need help finding your passion, visit **www.undefinableyou.com** by Dusti Arab.
- The Gallup-Healthways Well-Being Index is a fascinating

source of information on health and well-being: **www.well-beingindex.com**

- **Zenhabits.net** by Leo Babauta is "about finding simplicity in the daily chaos of our lives. It's about clearing the clutter so we can focus on what's important, create something amazing, find happiness."

Tiny House Resources

- Dee Williams and Katy Anderson designed and built my tiny house. You can find them at **PortlandAlternativeDwellings.com.**
- **www.relaxshacks.blogspot.com** by Derek Diedricksen.
- Looking for information on tiny homes? Visit the Small House Society: **www.resourcesforlife.com/small-house-society.**
- *TINY*, a documentary about tiny homes, will be released in spring 2012: **tiny-themovie.com.**
- **Tinyhouseblog.com** by Kent Griswold.
- **www.tinyhousedesign.com** by Michael Janzen.
- **Tinyrevolution.us** by Andrew Odom.
- **www.tumbleweedhouses.com** was founded by Jay Shafer.
- For current US building standards, see the International Building Code, **www.iccsafe.org**.

Index

G

H

I

J

K

L

M

S

T

U

V

W

Y

Z

About the Author

Photo by Logan Smith

Tammy Strobel is a writer, tiny house enthusiast, and coffee addict. She created her blog, RowdyKittens.com, in late 2007 to improve her writing and to share her story. Her story has been featured by the *New York Times*, *USA Today*, the *Today* show, CNN, MSNBC, and a variety of other media outlets.

Tammy spends her free time taking photos, volunteering, and hanging out with friends and family. She currently lives in a very tiny house in Portland, Oregon, with her husband, Logan, and two cats.

NEW WORLD LIBRARY is dedicated to publishing books and other media that inspire and challenge us to improve the quality of our lives and the world.

We are a socially and environmentally aware company, and we strive to embody the ideals presented in our publications. We recognize that we have an ethical responsibility to our customers, our staff members, and our planet.

We serve our customers by creating the finest publications possible on personal growth, creativity, spirituality, wellness, and other areas of emerging importance. We serve New World Library employees with generous benefits, significant profit sharing, and constant encouragement to pursue their most expansive dreams.

As a member of the Green Press Initiative, we print an increasing number of books with soy-based ink on 100 percent postconsumer-waste recycled paper. Also, we power our offices with solar energy and contribute to nonprofit organizations working to make the world a better place for us all.

Our products are available
in bookstores everywhere.
For our catalog, please contact:

New World Library
14 Pamaron Way
Novato, California 94949

Phone: 415-884-2100 or 800-972-6657
Catalog requests: Ext. 50
Orders: Ext. 52
Fax: 415-884-2199
Email: escort@newworldlibrary.com

To subscribe to our electronic newsletter, visit
www.newworldlibrary.com

3,147
trees were saved

HELPING TO PRESERVE OUR ENVIRONMENT

New World Library uses 100% postconsumer-waste recycled paper for our books whenever possible, even if it costs more. During 2011 this choice saved the following precious resources:

ENERGY	WASTEWATER	GREENHOUSE GASES	SOLID WASTE
22 MILLION BTU	600,000 GAL.	770,000 LB.	225,000 LB.

www.newworldlibrary.com

Environmental impact estimates were made using the Environmental Defense Fund Paper Calculator @ www.papercalculator.org.